CANFAKE

SELECTED WORKS BY DONALD WEBSTER

BOOKS

Early Slip-Decorated Pottery in Canada (1969)
Decorated Stoneware Pottery of North America (1971)
Early Canadian Pottery (1971)
The Book of Canadian Antiques (ed., 1974)
English-Canadian Furniture of the Georgian Period (1979)
Military Bolt Action Rifles: 1841–1918 (1993)

EXHIBITION CATALOGUES

American Country Furniture (1964)
Georgian Canada: Conflict and Culture, 1745–1820
(with Cross, Szylinger, 1984)
French-Canadian Furniture in the Royal Ontario Museum (1997)

ARCHAEOLOGICAL PAPERS

The Brantford Pottery, 1849–1907 (1968)
The William Eby Pottery, Conestogo, Ontario, 1855–1907 (1971)
Le domaine agricole d'un marchand aux XVIIe et XVIIIe siècles:
Le Site LeBer a l'île des Sœurs (ed., with Duguay, Pothier, 1994)

CANFAKE

AN EXPERT'S GUIDE TO THE TRICKS OF THE CANADIAN ANTIQUES TRADE

DONALD WEBSTER

Canadian Cataloguing in Publication Data

Webster, Donald Blake, 1933–
    Canfake : an expert's guide to the tricks of the Canadian antiques trade

Includes bibliographical references and index.
ISBN 0-7710-8904-X

1. Antiques – Expertising – Canada.   I. Title.

NK1125.W42 1997   745.1   C97-930026-6

The publishers acknowledge the support of the Canada Council and the Ontario Arts Council for their publishing program.

Typesetting by MacTrix DTP
Printed and bound in Canada

McClelland & Stewart Inc.
The Canadian Publishers
481 University Avenue
Toronto, Ontario
M5G 2E9

1 2 3 4 5   01 00 99 98 97

In memory of my eleven-times great-aunt, Hannah Emerson Dustin (1657–1731?), super-heroine or mass-murderess (depending on your viewpoint), whose turbulent era and harrowing exploits raised my original interest in history and antiquities.

Contents

Illustrations

Acknowledgements

As always the final words to be written, it becomes the duty and pleasure of every author of a project such as *Canfake* to thank all of those who have contributed, whether ideas, material, or necessary criticism. The initial idea for *Canfake* came some years ago, from a friend and collector of early coins, whom I shall leave nameless, who had been burned a few times by very good reproduction – and essentially fake – American colonial copper tokens. Over many years at the Royal Ontario Museum, then, I quietly began keeping a file on Canadian fakes, upgraded alterations, and reproductions passing as real. The file grew continually fatter, and I grew ever more amazed at the range and inventiveness of some of the fakery and scamming that was, and is, going on.

Even though much of the eventual draft manuscript was drawn from my own experience, or was my own opinion, I would still not have dared to publish it without testing the product with a few other readers of equal experience. To solicit a breadth of opinion, I enlisted Peter Kaellgren of the European Department of the ROM for another museum view. Clay Benson of Port Hope contributed his perspective from his many years as a professional antiques dealer. I also asked John Harbinson of Toronto, a major private collector, to offer comments from his viewpoint. For a perceptive but layperson's view, my wife, Ann, then went through two versions of the manuscript, clarifying terminology and jargon from a non-antiquarian perspective for the non-antiquarian reader.

I also invited two other dealers and one other collector to review and comment. So touchy is the subject of antiques fakery in its myriad variety that one declined altogether, saying I should just let sleeping dogs lie. The other two readers, though they also provided some valuable insights, asked to be left anonymous in these acknowledgements.

Finally, editor Pat Kennedy and copy editor Heather Sangster at McClelland & Stewart had the gruelling task of correcting my errors of grammar and syntax, and of spelling and punctuation. I thank and am greatly indebted to all, even though I did not, I must admit, follow all of everyone's comments or advice. Since the author always gets in the last word, the blame or derision for errors or misguided opinions must fall upon myself alone.

Once upon a time, when I was being introduced by lecture moderators as an "expert" in this or that, I had a tendency to believe them. No longer. The study of antiques and art involves analysis as much as evidence, and judgement as well as knowledge. In the infinite antiques world there are just too many unknowns, and always things which emerge as new, no matter one's accumulated knowledge or experience. Knowledge is never complete. There are no "experts," except those who have stopped learning, for observation, experience, and learning must be continuous, and antiquarians in any specialty are merely aging students.

Caledon, Ontario
January 1997

Introduction . . . and Some Definitions

"Contrariwise, if it was so, it might be; and if it were so, it would be; but as it isn't, it ain't. That's logic."
— Tweedledee, in Lewis Carroll's *Through the Looking-Glass*, 1872

A few years back, a friend of mine bought himself some isolated land and a small cottage on Ontario's French River, south of Sudbury. Barry had the cottage equipped with a propane stove and some kerosene lamps, but he still had to haul water from the river in a pail. He wanted a water pump, just a plain old small-sized, cast-iron water pump with a plain old up-down, up-down pump-handle, to mount beside his sink, with plastic tubing running to the river. He'd been looking for weeks. Figuring that cast-iron water pumps were a vanished thing of the pre-electrical past, he concentrated on country antiques shops. For weeks, no luck. The shops had just about everything *except* cast-iron water pumps. Ever in hope, Barry went to an antiques show on the outskirts of Toronto.

There, under a dealer's table, he found just the pump he wanted. It was small, painted blue, and fairly clean, not used much. He thought the asking price was crazy: $150. Still, $150 for an antique water pump was better than forever carrying buckets of water, so he bought it. He then discovered that the leather suction seal was so dried out and desiccated that he had to get a new one specially made – for another $50.

Barely a month later, his wife was cleaning out a stack of magazines and catalogues, including a Canadian Tire catalogue that had come in

1

the mail. Barry hadn't looked at it, but he now riffled through it, and there, lo and behold, was a plain cast-iron water pump. Not only was the pump in the catalogue picture also blue, but in every detail it looked *exactly* like the water pump he had bought and equipped with a new suction seal. Canadian Tire wanted $39.95 for their brand-new pump, a living antique still being made, which they carried just for people with cottages that did not yet have electricity.

Antiques seem to have been around, and have been collected, ever since people began making objects many millennia ago and those objects began to survive the life spans of their makers and users. Fakes and forgeries seem to have followed collecting ever since people discovered the concept of value and began to accumulate physical objects.

Given Barry and his water pump, however, we have to begin by asking just *what is* an antique. The very term "antique" is rather loose and imprecise, with broad meanings subject to interpretation. The American Webster's dictionary definition, other than referring to classical antiquity, is: "of, or in the style of, a former period," "a piece of furniture, silverware, etc., made in a former period, generally more than a hundred years ago." The English Oxford dictionary definition is also imprecise, including: "aged, ancient, olden," "old-fashioned; out of date," and "having existed since olden times." Only the Webster's definition mentions a particular age, one hundred years, but since it is an American dictionary, that probably reflects only the U.S. Customs definition.

All dictionary definitions of "antique" or "antiquity" refer solely to age, as do the Canadian and U.S. customs definitions for duty-free status for antiques. For Canadian Customs, the duty-free age depends on the classification of a particular object. Basically, the required age for antique status is one hundred years, but that has now been reduced to fifty years for many classifications. For Canadian-made objects, previously exported and returning to Canada, the antique age is twenty-five years, and for antique cars, until the coming of NAFTA, the age was fifteen years.

The American definition of a duty-free antique was set at one hundred years in and as of 1930. Rather than specifying a hundred years, however, with the age to advance each year, Congress instead set a date for the end of antiquity: January 1, 1830. To be allowed duty-free status, imported antiques thus had to get older and older, to over a hundred and thirty years when the law was finally changed to a firm hundred years in the 1960s. The American duty-free "antiques" definition remains at one hundred years of age, for all categories. Objects of American origin, however, can return to the country duty-free at any age.

From even a superficial look at the real world of the Canadian antiques and collector market and what it actually includes, however, it is clear that the old hundred-year age definition of "antique" disappeared in practice many years ago. Market realities have virtually abandoned age definitions of "antique." The definition has now become so much more flexible – or so debased and distorted, depending on one's viewpoint – that three quite separate and different definitions of "antique" now seem to be current. They are simply a pulling together, my own sort of synthesis, from many years of observation, and I will refer to them further. All three are fairly flexible, even loose, but they can be distilled as follows.

Definition-1: An antique is something that somewhat, but not strictly, follows the Canadian or American customs specific age definitions, with an age of either one hundred or fifty years, depending on the object classification. In the antiques market, however, Definition-1 seems to depend less on age than on types of objects, but still has quite fluid limits. Definition-1 basically covers individually or handmade *craft-period* objects, even though they may be more recent than one hundred years. Definition-1 seems to stop, though – or Definition-1 dealers and collectors seem to balk – before getting into factory-manufactured and *industrial-period* objects, even though they may be older than one hundred years. This, however, is not rigid. The Canadian upper-level and higher-value antiques market, probably less than 10 per cent of the total, seems to focus primarily on earlier craft-period rather than manufactured objects, and operates largely according to Definition-1.

Definition-2: An antique in this category is any object that has not been in general or common use within the life span of most still-living people. This is a middle ground and also a loose definition, which accommodates both later craft-period as well as earlier manufactured objects. The minimum age for Definition-2 antiques now appears to be about seventy-five to eighty years, or pieces dating roughly from before the beginning of the First World War. Some dealers – particularly those who specialize in later-nineteenth- and early-twentieth-century furniture, glass, and ceramics – seem to operate by Definition-2.

Definition-3: An antique here is just about any object that can no longer be manufactured or produced, is gone from general consumer retail markets, and is no longer in common present-day use. Barry's water pump would fall under this category. Under Definition-3, some objects can become antique as soon as they can no longer be acquired new – or even not *readily* be acquired new. Ephemeral things, such as disposable containers – wooden boxes, metal cans, and glass bottles – or other throw-aways, such as car licence plates, political election buttons, or swizzle sticks and matchbooks from defunct bars, would head this list.

Other objects, it seems, must await obsolescence and a longer-term throw-away period, perhaps ten to twenty years, to qualify for antique status. My ancient 1985 computer, or our even-more-geriatric TV, would fall into this category. The life span during which most objects produced today are in common use is hardly greater than that, and often it is shorter. At least 90 per cent of the Canadian antiques market, and that in the United States as well, now seems to operate largely on a basis of Definition-3, accepting merely obsolete objects as antiques (or "collectibles").

Now that we have the term "antique" elaborated on and fully confused, let's move on to the terms "fake" and "reproduction," the main subjects of this book.

The Webster's dictionary defines "fake" as: "to make [something] seem real, satisfactory, etc. by any sort of deception; practice deception by simulating or tampering with [something]; counterfeit," and also "fraudulent; not genuine; sham; false." Oxford is less precise, with: "to tamper with, for the purpose of deception," and also "a piece of manipulation." Both the Webster and Oxford definitions of "fake" include the mention of intent to deceive, and both definitions could also apply to a lot of present-day reproductions.

W. G. Constable, in his *Forgers and Forgeries* (1954), put this very succinctly, coming up with a better definition than either dictionary.

> The usual idea of a [fake or] forgery is something deliberately fabricated to appear to be what it is not; something conceived in sin, and carrying the taint of illegitimacy throughout its existence. In fact, however, many things made for quite innocent and even laudable purposes [reproductions] have been used to deceive and defraud, by means of misrepresentation or subsequent manipulation. So the essential element in forgery lies in the way an object is presented, rather than in the purpose that inspired its making.

Given the nature of the Canadian antiques market, however, Constable missed the point that a fake or forgery can also be and often is "presented" in ignorance, quite innocently and with no *intent* to "deceive and defraud." Dealers can be just as lacking in knowledge as buyer-collectors, and can quite innocently include faked or reproduction pieces in their inventories. So can even the most upscale auction houses. The fake is still both a fake and a fraud, except that the fraud began with some previous transaction and, however unknowingly, has simply been carried forward through sale after sale.

A reproduction, by the Webster's definition, is "a copy, likeness, or reconstruction" that "implies an exact or very close imitation of an existing thing." A reproduction eventually becomes an antique in its own right, simply through the passage of time, though it also remains a reproduction *as long as* it is known to be and is offered and sold as a reproduction. The minute it is "presented," or offered, or sold as an older and original piece, it immediately also becomes a fake. That status of fake continues until or unless the piece is re-identified and goes back to being designated as a reproduction. Figures 26 and 27 show just such pieces.

Hardly all Canadian antiques collectors focus only on objects of Canadian origin or with some Canadian historical connection. In fact, probably only a minority do. Collectors' tastes and desires range worldwide, from Latin American silver to Spanish majolica pottery, from

Chinese snuff bottles to Japanese carved netsuke, or from theatre pro-
grams to myriad types of nineteenth-century barbed wire. There are
absolutely no limits to collecting tastes and desires.

Fakes and reproductions have emerged with just about every object
or art form that has ever been produced or collected, and at present is
too great a subject for any single book. This book, instead, is focused
on the Canadian antiques market and how it works, and on fakes,
fakery, and reproductions of solely Canadian objects. There are plenty.
Some of the types of fakes that emerge in Canadian antiques are similar
to the same types around the world; others seem quite unique to
Canada. Fakery, and the making of reproductions, however, is largely
motivated by money everywhere, and is created and sustained by
market demand. Unless there is a market, and some profit in it for the
producers, the making of fakes and reproductions would not exist.

It is impossible to know today what or how many "antique" objects,
including even some from the Definition-3 1940s and 1950s, are still
being made as living antiques (like cast-iron water pumps) or have
been reproduced over the past fifty years. It is almost easier today to
think of what *has not* been reproduced. I suspect the answer to that is,
by now, close to nothing. Nearly every time I see something in the
antiques market that I suspect has never been reproduced, I end up sur-
prised. Along comes still another reproductions catalogue and, as if
risen from the dead, there it is.

There is nothing wrong with antique reproductions, as long as they
remain identifiable and stay defined as such. Many reproductions,
because of style, materials, or differences in construction from the
original pieces, will always be identifiable. An ever-increasing number,
however – because of reasonable exactness of reproduction combined
with the ignorance of many buyers – at some stage enter the antiques
market as original pieces. These pieces may well circulate as genuine
forever, unless they are identified by someone who knows better.

Even so, their identification does not necessarily mean that reproductions, or fakes, will be removed from the antiques market. Most
people meeting a suspicious piece will just quietly pass on buying,
without comment. And if someone does comment, so what? Even if

the seller temporarily sets the piece aside, sooner or later it will resurface. Thus, most fakes or misrepresented reproductions simply remain in the market until they find another home, as if they had never been discovered.

Except for saying that any dealer, generically, is someone who buys and sells, what an antiques dealer actually is, or does, cannot be any more precisely defined than can an "antique." No one knows the number or variety of antiques dealers in Canada. Full-time dealers, or at least those who maintain shops and/or advertise in antiques-market magazines, are listed in annual directories published in some provinces. At a rough guess I would say there are probably three thousand to five thousand listed dealers across the country.

As well as dealers with shops, there are also many part-time players and a lot of turnover among people moving in and out of the antiques market. Beyond full-time dealers, the most successful of which stay in business for decades, there are probably ten or twenty times as many other players, from private dealers with specialized clientele to pickers and picker-auctioneers to flea-market-booth holders. Even dealers with shops, and who advertise, are not necessarily full-time dealers. Neither do they always open and staff their shops during their own absences, whether they are also employed elsewhere or off on buying trips. Many dealers very aptly advertise that they are open only on weekends or "by appointment or by chance."

So, antiques collectors are just one ingredient in a very mixed stew. Collectors face loose definitions and standards, a world of completely open and unrestricted wheeling and dealing; real minefields of games, tricks, pitfalls, and scams; honest and dishonest mistakes; and innocent and ignorant misrepresentations as well as deliberate ones. In between the lines, they sometimes also discover absolute treasures and, occasionally, real bargains or "sleepers." With antiques, fakes, reproductions, dealers, collectors, and the whole anarchy of the antiques market itself, I can only think of that old saying: "Things are not always what they seem."

The grand game of antiques collecting is often as close as one can come, in a non-violent if not necessarily peaceful way, to a blood sport.

Les antiquaires.

Fig. 1: Antiquarians are a cynical lot, but only as they must be. "*Les antiquaires,*" a French lithograph of the 1840s, is a caricature of five obviously experienced and competitive antiquarians examining a box of coins and small trinkets. All of the expressions of curiosity, questioning, scrutiny, intensity, and suspicion illustrate perfectly the knowledge, experience, and careful judgement that must be applied by present-day antiquarians and collectors. Then or now, in the antiques world some things never change. *Author files*

An archaeological colleague, Ivor Noel Hume, in his book *All the Best Rubbish* (1974), put this very nicely:

> There can be no denying that value has much to do with the collecting instinct, for once two people want the same object it acquires a commercial price. Here it is that we differ from our animal cousins; they have no means of obtaining their neighbors' treasures short of theft or mayhem. We first try trading. Competition is a basic element of the collector's makeup, and the competitive spirit, as everyone knows, is thoroughly praiseworthy and should be fostered in every contributing member of society from Cub Scouts and baton-twirling moppets to football-playing assassins. In the world of collecting, this healthy philosophy is often tastefully interpreted as "screwing the dealer." It is, fortunately, a sufficiently reciprocal pursuit as to retain the essential element of sportsmanship.

To many collectors, the hunt and the chase is often more important than the ultimate catch. To others, the catch, and possession by whatever means, is the only goal. In a game without rules, the bottom line comes down to everyone trying to outwit everyone else. Accumulated observation, study, knowledge, and experience (which I will push *ad nauseum* in the following pages) provide both protective armour and weapons.

Thus, the real purpose of this book is to explore the jungle of the antiques world, and its flora and fauna, with live-action tales of true adventures along the way. If all (or any) of this can help would-be, novice, or even experienced collectors, traders, or dealers navigate the jungle without getting tangled in the vines, the exercise will have been worth it.

Have fun!

1

Into the Jungle:
The Canadian Antiques Market

———◆◆◇◆◆———

*"Then I saw that wisdom excelleth folly, as far as light excelleth darkness.
The wise man's eyes are in his head; but the fool walketh in darkness."*
— *Ecclesiastes* 2:13, 14

Forty years ago, fakery of Canadian antiques was a non-problem. Interest in antiques collecting was at a very primitive level, and only a handful of far-sighted specialist collectors were building Canadian antiques collections, at what was then quite a low cost. When the market for Canadian antiques was small in the 1920s to the 1940s, with many superb and genuine Canadian pieces still readily available and prices relatively low, there was little point in faking anything. English and European fakes and reproductions were a different matter (see Appendix One), and had been entering Canada for decades.

That situation has changed. Interest in antiques collecting has grown massively in the past few decades. Books have been written and published, and specialized magazines established. Major auction houses have grown and prospered. Hundreds of antiques shops have opened, and at least one antiques show is held somewhere every weekend in the year.

Price appreciation has more than kept pace with the growth of the antiques market. Finer and rarer examples of painting, furniture, silver, and pottery have gradually disappeared into both private and museum collections, leaving ever less in the way of genuine pieces available on the market at any particular time.

Growth of the antiques market in Canada, combined with the ever-declining availability of finer pieces, has driven prices constantly upward and has encouraged both fakery and, to a much greater extent, a sizeable trade in look-alike reproductions. The making of fakes and the manufacturing of reproductions is purely economic; it is simply makers seizing economic opportunities to increase supplies to fill market demands. Collectors and museums in countries with much longer antiquities collecting experiences than Canada have faced fakery for centuries, but it is a fairly new phenomena in this country – and growing.

Before getting into fakery, however, it is necessary first to look at antiques collecting from the aspects of exactly what makes value, what drives the antiques market, and what motivates fakes and reproductions. Whatever it is that creates value is also certainly the core rationale for fakery. For that matter, why are antiques valuable at all, instead of being considered just battered and tatty old stuff? Why, as well, are some objects so much more valuable than others that are very similar?

Virtually everything that possibly could be collected is collected now by someone and, often, by many people. In certain subject areas there are now enough collectors of specific types of objects to sustain many North American or worldwide collectors' associations, and sometimes even specialized magazines or newsletters. Though the collecting of some objects might seem pretty silly to most people, it is not always just a symptom of human acquisitiveness. A lot of collecting, and particularly that which involves spending substantial amounts of money on objects, is also value-oriented and a form of speculative capital investment. Thus, many collectors, whatever their aesthetic, scholarly, or decorative motivations, also have hopes of eventual capital gain.

That raises some key questions. Are Canadian antiques, or antiques generally, a good capital investment? Are future price values likely to rise sufficiently to beat cumulative inflation and not only provide some ultimate real (beyond inflation) gain, but perhaps even beat stock and bond markets and long-term investment indexes? No matter what other motivations they may have for collecting, those are questions some collectors keep in the backs of their minds with every buying or selling decision.

It is very difficult to get a firm feel or a valid impression of the broader antiques market. It is composed solely of individuals, myriad players all following their own varied motives and preferences, and their own definitions of "antique." The market is not really an industry, like manufacturing or farming, in any sense of uniformity of product or market. Neither is it a categorized (or probably even categorizable) area of economic activity. There are no agreed upon or uniform definitions or standards, no imposed regulations, and, particularly, no hard figures or statistics. Though the art and antiques market is economically motivated and driven, no one knows its scale, size, or its impact on the Gross Domestic Product in Canada, nor would these probably even be measurable.

One thing is obvious. The antiques market is one of the last pure supply-and-demand situations left and, except for taxes, is subject to very little government regulation or interference. It is a market, in fact, that is so unorganized, so essentially an anarchy, that it is not really amenable to regulation; it is beyond regulation. It is also a multi-tentacled market that, on the bottom line, operates on a basis of direct individual transactions, which themselves call for knowledge, wits, caution, and decisiveness.

As well, the antiques market, as might be expected of any complex and uncontrollable activity, is full of pitfalls for the ignorant or unwary, the careless or the foolish. Anarchy that it is, the market abounds with games and tricks, and even deliberate scams. Preservation of reputations is perhaps the prime inhibitor of true fraud, but there is a lot of shadowy activity and skating on thin ice, and ethics are not a first priority.

The antiques market, and collecting, is also a grand sport, a mental combat game like chess, Monopoly, or blackjack, in which everyone seeks advantage or is trying to outwit everyone else. Therefore, personal knowledge, awareness, and experience, as in any other field, is the greatest attribute any collector can have. Knowledge is an absolute requisite to survival.

There are two key concepts to remember in the antiques market. The first is *caveat emptor*, or buyer beware, the Latin term meaning that the buyer takes the risk. In a market with few real guarantees of anything – and little effective recourse for sour transactions – *caveat emptor* means that if a buyer pays too much for something, or buys a fake or faked-up piece, it's his or her own fault for not knowing better. Pure and deliberate fraud is fairly rare, but the level of ignorance among many dealers and buyers is also such that anything can happen.

The second concept is that of "one last buyer." In an anarchical market with no guarantees, both dealers and collectors, rather than trying to seek recourse from a seller, instead have a tendency simply to unload their mistakes. No matter how much they may have overpaid for something, or however faked or made-up a piece may be, the "one last buyer" concept means that there is always another dupe. There is always someone out there somewhere, every bit as ignorant as they were, who would be willing to pay more or who can be conned into taking a questionable piece.

There are also no price-value standards in the antiques market, or any but the most approximate of value guides or sales track records. As I outlined earlier, the term "antique" is also a bit of a misnomer, for it refers solely to age, though age alone has probably the least influence on collector interest or on actual object values. A great many people, in fact, collect semi-modern objects, perhaps out of nostalgia for their own youth. Thus, age by itself, and just the natural attrition of objects that occurs with the passage of time, may create eventual scarcity or even rarity, but, to repeat, age alone has very little to do with antique values. There are many old, and even ancient, objects that are essentially valueless (Figs. 2, 3).

In a supply-and-demand market, values are created instead by current collector demand, and only by current collector demand. Are there more collectors at any particular time who want specific objects or categories of objects than there are pieces available, or is the availability of the objects greater than the demand for them?

The actual number of antique objects that may still exist is much less relevant in determining value than the number that might be *available at any particular time.* For example, probably some hundreds of Quebec eighteenth-century diamond-point-panelled armoires or

Fig. 2: Age may make something antique, but age by itself has little to do with values or prices. On the left is a section of an ancient Roman–British flue tile, of about 350 A.D., excavated from a public bath on Thames Street, London. On the right is a five-hundred-year-old pottery-kiln saggar, dating from roughly 1450, an archaeological find from a medieval pottery at Wakefield, Yorkshire. Since there is no collector or market demand for such pottery segments, no matter how antique they may be, in market terms today these ancient pieces are worthless. *Author's collection*

Fig. 3: This is another illustration of the fact that age alone has little bearing on antique values, but condition has a major influence. The upper two of these four eighteenth-century English copper coins are long-circulated half-pennies, a George I piece of 1718 on the left, and a George III half-penny, dated 1774. The lower pair are, or were, George III pennies of the later eighteenth century. Both obviously circulated for many decades and are worn so smooth that the dates are indecipherable. No matter their antiquity, these coins are valueless because of their extremely poor condition. *Author's collection*

low buffets still exist (even wholly genuine ones), but most are already in collections and thus are not available or presently for sale. Demand, however, is always high in relation to the number of diamond-point armoires that are available *at any single time*. Thus, the value trend is always upwards – even if there are not that many prospective buyers or pieces available. If only one original, genuine, untouched, and unfaked diamond-point armoire is available for sale, and four collectors want it, that is enough. Those are exactly the conditions that can generate very high prices, which in turn make fakery and reproductions worthwhile.

The Collectors and Dealers

Antiques collecting has evolved and expanded from a quite elitist pursuit in the post-First World War period through the 1930s to a very populist and popularized pastime in the half-century-plus since the Second World War. Part of this perhaps has to do with great postwar economic expansion and increasing personal incomes. The influences of the growth of home-decorating magazines, of expanding newspapers with "Women's," "Life," or "Arts" sections that include antiques columnists, and of television have also been at least as great.

Certainly an equally great boost in the popularizing of antiques collecting has been the growth of historic houses and re-created historical-village museums, composed of collected and restored early buildings. The buildings are then furnished with carefully selected original and compatible objects, from furniture and lighting to tools and rugs. Before the Second World War there were no such sites in Canada. Since then, historical-village museums, such as Upper Canada Village or Black Creek Pioneer Village, in Ontario, or King's Landing, in New Brunswick, have proliferated. There are now dozens, large and small, all across Canada, and every schoolchild and virtually the entire adult population has visited at least one at least once. The historical-village museums developed over the past fifty years have, for the first time, allowed great numbers of people to see and even handle large numbers of antiques in a relatively natural and reasonably accurate environment. As a result, these museums have been one of the strongest influences in stimulating antiques collecting.

Largely, collectors can be divided into three categories: "generalist," "specialist," and "rarefied" (or elitist). Their various collecting motives, outlooks, approaches, and goals are as different as winter and summer.

The great majority of Canadian collectors (probably 70 or 80 per cent) – the main customers of the antiques dealers and auction houses – are usually furnishing and decorating homes or cottages or simply collecting objects that appeal to their acquisitive senses in a very general way. They are the market-dominant category of "generalist" collectors, with very broad interests but little specific focus. While they form the largest market, they are also, by "specialist" or "rarefied" standards, a rather unsophisticated group.

Generalist collectors have varied and often wide-ranging tastes, but usually no considerable knowledge. They may perhaps have a few broad-spectrum or "coffee-table" books on antiques or home decorating, but hardly a sizeable library. They are the collectors who often go for stripped pine "country" furniture, simpler levels of "folk" art, or ordinary redware and stoneware pottery crocks and jugs.

As well, generalists are typically fashion- and decor-oriented, rather than specifically object-oriented, which is what separates them from the specialists. The generalists are often seeking antiques as part of home-decorating projects, rather than as objects in themselves. They will sometimes even spot a location in their homes first and then go browsing for something to fill that spot. Many specialized and rarefied collectors, of course, do not even recognize generalists as "collectors," but instead consider them simply as accumulators.

Generalists are the typical subscribers to glossy, large-circulation decor-oriented magazines, such as *Canadian Homes* or *Century Homes*, rather than to object-oriented collector magazines, such as *Antiques!*, *Antique Showcase*, or the American *The Magazine Antiques* or *The Connoisseur*. Because it is oriented to decor rather than objects, this is also the market most prone to ignorance-based mistakes.

Generalist collectors are also usually in the lower economic end of the market, and will not typically spend a great deal of money on any single piece. This puts most generalists into the Definition-2 or -3 antiques market, but not usually into the more rarefied and expensive Definition-1. Because of this, generalist collectors also make up the prime market for contemporary reproductions. Specialist and rarefied collectors are far more focused and purist, and are after only original and genuine pieces.

Since a significant percentage of the collector market is in this generalist and Definition-2 or -3 category, their interests colour what most dealers, whether country antiques-shop owners or flea-market sellers, prefer to handle. The generalists, particularly, influence what dealers will pay for something. If a dealer knows that his or her customers are largely Sunday-afternoon generalists, with a fairly low or moderate limit on what they will spend, then that dealer is also not likely to risk spending many thousands of dollars on rare or fine single pieces. Except by accident, he or she would lack access to a rarefied or connoisseur market for them. That dealer, instead, is far better off keeping an inventory of numerous but lower-priced pieces and leaving the rare and supreme to the minority of specialist dealers and collectors.

The great majority of Canadian dealers are therefore as generalist as the majority of their customers. Their shops may include almost anything, for they are catering at the same time to decor-oriented generalists, impulse buyers, and object-dedicated and single-focus collectors. They try to include and mix in something for everyone, and many such shops enjoy a heavy traffic of browsers, whatever their actual sales.

The dividing line between dealers and collectors is so murky that it can be difficult to define just what a dealer is. Dealers, of course, buy and sell, but so do many active collectors. For that matter, some dealers are also collectors, keeping their own collections separate from their inventories.

Probably only a minority of dealers are full time, making a living solely in antiques dealing. As mentioned earlier, most, instead, are part-time dealers, some with shops open only on weekends or by appointment. Still others are mixed collector-dealers, who have no shops and exhibit and sell only at antique shows. Private dealers, also part time and often in rarefied specialties, may exhibit at a few antiques shows, but operate mainly by networking, and sell largely by phone and fax to a small clientele.

Very few dealers specialize solely in Canadian antiques, nor can they, for the potential buyer base is too small. Instead, most are much broader in their offerings, though they may be strongest in particular subject niches in which they have a special interest. Many dealers may try to focus on some particular broad area, such as English furniture or European ceramics, but few will concentrate exclusively on that.

The minority, the 20 or 30 per cent of collectors and dealers who are true specialists, are primarily object-oriented rather than fashion- or decor-oriented, and most focus on specific categories of objects. They pursue their collecting or dealing, or both, with very deliberate goals, always looking for pieces they lack. Though a minority, specialists, focusing on some single category of object – whether stamps or coins, antique tools, early ceramics or glass, mechanical toys, or obsolete beer cans – are also the most dedicated to their collecting.

The rarefied category of specialist collectors – those who collect early silver, historical paintings, stylized Georgian-Canadian furniture or furniture from New France, antique guns, and other rarities – are an even-more-limited group. They probably account for no more than 5 per cent, and probably less, of the entire collector population. They also occupy the top echelon, largely because of superior knowledge and superior finances. Both are necessary to be able to compete for and afford the finer and rarer – and often very expensive – categories of objects they may be after.

The specialist collectors, in being the most dedicated, are always seeking, and they know exactly what they are seeking. The generalists often do not, until they see it. Specialists are scanners. Whether they are pottery, tool, glass, licence-plate, or pocketknife collectors, specialists can often eyeball and get a feel for an antiques shop or a show booth from the entrance, and with instant intuition know whether it is worth perusing more closely. The generalist, on the other hand, will typically enter first and then browse, often buying on impulse. An experienced dealer can usually spot whether a potential customer is a focused specialist or a browsing generalist.

Specialist collectors and dealers are also likely to have extensive libraries on their chosen subjects, and typically will have greater knowledge than the generalist dealers or auction houses from whom they often buy. Some are also antiquarian scholars, researching, comparing, and seeking knowledge in addition to pieces for their own collections. Thus, specialist scholar-collectors, museum curators, and dealers often write articles and books on antiques, and become the acknowledged authorities.

Specialist dealers also usually have their own antiquarian interests beyond buying and selling. It can even be said that some specialized dealers are at heart just doubly focused collectors, and their own collections and sometimes even their household furnishings come and go a lot. A particularly assiduous dealer I know once sold the connubial bed right from under her napping husband, leaving their mattress on the floor until she found another bed.

Specialist dealers pick a particular subject category and market niche, and deal for the most part only in that category.

Just within Canada, antique tools, lamps and lighting fixtures, architectural and building ornaments and details, glass, firearms, beds, early tools and agricultural implements, coins and stamps, militaria, silver, precision instruments, antique jewellery, rare books, pottery, textiles, horse-drawn vehicles, antique woodstoves, and many other categories, down to sports cards, postcards, sheet music, comic books, and movie memorabilia, all have subject-specialized collectors and dealers.

Being in special-focus and niche markets of antiques, most specialized dealers also have well-developed buyer-collector bases, often continent-wide, and personally know many of their specialist collector customers. Since niche-market specialized dealers often do most of their business through lists and catalogues, by mail order, many do not even need or have retail shops.

The collections of specialists, quite the opposite of those of the generalists, often have little or nothing to do with either fashion or home furnishing and decor. Their collections may even live hidden away in cabinets or vaults, or in special lockable collection rooms set aside in their homes. I know one specialist collector, an orthopaedic surgeon, who collects medieval swords and daggers, his earliest dating from about 1250. Given the rarity and worldwide collector-demand factor, collecting ancient swords and daggers can be a very expensive pastime, and one that exposes the collector to a lot of past fakery and alteration, some of it centuries old. His collection, because of its value, rests in locked steel cabinets. Beyond that, the surgeon's wife is also a dedicated peace activist who will not have anything that resembles weaponry visible anywhere in their house.

The Market Structure

In antiques of any category, the value differences between the typical and common, and the excellent and rare, are dramatic. For example, a plain small pine table (Fig. 4) or dry sink, or a late-nineteenth-century piece of table silver, can easily sell for under $500 and has a potential market and buyer base of many thousands of people. The generalist collectors, though perhaps at the low-value end of the market, because of their numbers also provide the bread and butter of the Canadian antiques market.

Conversely, a truly fine and rare piece of eighteenth-century serving silver by one of the more famous early Montreal makers, or a splendid carved and labelled 1820s mahogany table by Thomas Nisbet (Figs. 5, 5a), selling at perhaps $20,000, has a potential market of certainly no more than twenty to thirty collectors in all of Canada. Few dealers or collectors are either that cognizant of stylized and formal Canadian pieces, or are in that financial league. Thus, the appreciation and market for the top-most and rarest level of Canadian antiques is extremely narrow.

A private and part-time dealer who specializes in silver and knows all of the serious collectors has told me that, for a piece of Canadian antique silver selling for over $5,000, his potential market of dedicated collectors – people he would call or fax about the piece – numbers about twenty. Though there are several thousand individual antiques

Fig. 4: Simple pine tables, which were often just sawed boards nailed and pinned together, were multi-purpose kitchen pieces, present in every early household. They received heavy use and abuse, and most of these tables have been repaired or altered in one way or another. The angled top corners of this piece, for example, were cut much later than the making of the table itself. Many have survived, and thus such tables today, usually stripped of any original paint or finish and "tarted up," are among the commonest forms of nineteenth-century furniture. This table, perhaps a little more elaborate than many, with its hinged top, turned legs, and lower drawer, is a generic Quebec table of the mid-nineteenth century. In the antiques market it would be valued at roughly $500, with the usual pricing spread depending on where and how it might be sold. *Private collection*

Fig. 5: Thomas Nisbet of Saint John, New Brunswick, was one of the finest early Canadian cabinetmakers, and over two hundred of his labelled pieces are now known. With its carved and rope-twist legs, this mahogany table is a good example of Nisbet's work of the early 1820s. Since labelled Nisbet furniture is now almost all in museum or private collections, and pieces only rarely appear for sale, an elegant table such as this would probably bring $20,000 or more at auction. It would also be among the perhaps only 5 per cent of Canadian antiques with good long-term investment potential. *Royal Ontario Museum*

Fig. 5a: Thomas Nisbet was one of only four early Canadian cabinetmakers who labelled at least some of his furniture. There are enough known labelled pieces to provide a good body of evidence, so that the style and workmanship can be compared with other unlabelled examples to make reliable attributions. The Nisbet label in several versions was rather roughly printed on rag paper and pasted on the undersides or insides of drawers of tables. Most labels have become discoloured, dry, and flaky with age, and this example is in much better condition than most. *Royal Ontario Museum*

dealers and shops in Canada, there are also perhaps not fifty dealers in the country who could or would dare invest $10,000 to $20,000 or more in a single piece of Canadian silver or furniture.

I have said earlier that the broader and generalist Canadian antiques market is unsophisticated, a condition which tends to overvalue the typical, ordinary, or even crude, and undervalues the fine and elegant. This ignorance, of course, can also lead to knowledgeable buyers finding occasional real bargains in fine or rare pieces. It is difficult to pin down the psychology behind this, but there seem to be some multiple but interconnected background causes.

One reason for this cultural short-sightedness perhaps lies with the historical and social correctness that is force-fed to every Canadian schoolchild. Kicked off and reinforced by the capital-C Centennial of Confederation in 1967, with its own dollar bill and its government-sponsored version of national awareness, most Canadians are conditioned to view Confederation as the Dawn of Creation. The two and a half Canadian centuries that came before 1867, or the 150 years of English–French Wars, or the fact that Confederation was actually Canada's fifth constitution, are all part of a sort of Dark Ages, superficially realized and less understood.

Michele Landsberg, in her *Toronto Star* column, once wrote that Canada was such a peace-loving nation that no war had ever been fought on Canadian soil. If that represents the general state of Canadian historical awareness, then it is little wonder that the average consciousness of Canadian cultural development extends about as far back as the last federal election, or that scraped and refinished pine dry sinks, kitchen tables, simple cupboards, or pressed-back chairs are the "antiques" preference of most generalist collectors.

A parallel correctness, emphasized in the schools to the level of mythology, is the great pioneer syndrome. Every immigrant to early Canada, it seems, became a sterling, strong-hearted pioneer. The pioneers occupied land grants, cleared forests, built log cabins and solid homemade furniture to put in them, eventually established prosperous farms, and did Generally Good Things. No one seemed to settle in towns, establish manufacturing industries, open retail stores, trade in commodities, speculate in real estate, pull shady financial deals, rob or thieve, inhabit taverns, ever get drunk or play around with other than their spouse, or was anything, God forbid, but an upstanding, hard-working, law-abiding, temperate, and church-going citizen. The strong-hearted pioneer syndrome has been grossly overstressed, but its popular culture and imagery still very substantially colours popular preferences in antiques and reinforces the scraped-pine mainstream of the Canadian antiques market.

Within Canada, the French-speaking Québécois seem to have the greatest feeling of historical awareness. As with many Europeans and Britons, the Québécois innately seem to know where they are from and who they are. So do a great many Americans, though perhaps that is courtesy of very different and much more nationalistic correctness in the schools.

It seems to be largely this combination of school-fed images – Confederation-as-Creation and the sterling-pioneer syndrome – that has conditioned a low-level and sometimes mythological historical and cultural awareness; the two are complementary. Thus, settler-pioneers, who in reality were subsistence-level farmers and woodcutters on the lower rungs of early society, are venerated. At the same time, Canadians recognize few great national accomplishments or achievers and have no national heroes.

This means, with antiques, that the ordinary and mediocre are typically overvalued, both aesthetically and economically, while the fine or significant are substantially undervalued. In this sense, the Canadian antiques market is unlike that of any other country. This also seems to distort what really makes value in an antiquity: original quality, rarity, and collector demand.

As another unusual factor, Canadian art and antiques – unlike those of Britain, France, China, or Japan – with little exception have a following and a market only within Canada. To be sure, a very few historical artists, such as Cornelius Krieghoff, or contemporary artists, such as Jean-Paul Riopelle, Michael Snow, Paul-Émile Borduas, or Alex Colville, have international reputations and markets. Others, such as Ontario's Group of Seven, have limited international recognition and, even within Canada, a largely regional Ontario market. The finest of Canadian historical furniture, even the stylized and elegant early Montreal and Maritimes mahogany, has no international and even pitifully little Canadian recognition as such. Early Canadian silver is the same as art and furniture, with minimal international recognition and only a very small Canadian collector base.

Much early Canadian furniture, in styles and woods, is very similar to American or English furniture. Because of the demand and the price disparities, or lack of Canadian collector interest, great quantities of finer Canadian furniture have been trucked to the United States over the years, to lose Canadian identity and gain American nationality. Many pieces are now in the American antiques market, masquerading as American furniture, and more leaves every month.

Early American furniture, of course, also occasionally appears in the Canadian antiques market. Some probably came with heavy post-Loyalist and nineteenth-century immigration, and more by way of dealer imports. This furniture often appears with hazy Canadian provenances and even attributions, and by American price standards sometimes presents real bargains.

The fact that upper-level Canadian art and antiques for the most part have only a Canadian market, and a small and narrow one at that, severely depresses market values. This shows clearly in comparative price levels. In furniture, a very few French-Canadian and Ontario-German pieces have sold privately in the range of $50,000 and up. One Quebec New France-period three-drawer commode sold for $100,000 in 1989. No single piece of early Canadian fine and elegant mahogany furniture, however, even a maker-labelled piece, has yet to exceed $30,000.

In the United States, almost any fine piece of furniture that is either labelled or reliably attributed to a famous maker is likely to exceed US$100,000. Since 1976 at least seven American pieces have topped $1 million at auction. The most expensive piece of American furniture so far was a rare 1760s Newport (Rhode Island) mahogany secretary-bookcase, sold at auction in 1989 for $12.1 million. No piece of early Canadian furniture has yet exceeded the $100,000 paid for the Quebec commode.

In silver, fine British and American examples by well-known makers such as Hester Bateman, Paul Storr, or Paul Revere II will regularly bring $50,000 or more at auction, and elaborate pieces regularly pass $100,000. Only one piece – actually a rare 1790s four-piece set – of Canadian silver has ever sold for over $25,000 at auction, and 99 per cent sells for far less. Canadian nineteenth-century spoons marked by well-known makers can readily be had for under $100.

Some fine and rare examples of both British and American ceramics have gone for well over $100,000 at auction, and a few have reached $250,000. Only the most rare of Canadian pottery will bring over $1,000, and the record price so far for a piece of Canadian pottery was just over $12,000.

In an auction sale, the immediate effect on prices of buyer demand and competition is obvious. If three people are bidding on the same piece, they will drive the price up in less than a minute, until the successful bidder is the last one to stay in. On the other hand, if only one person bids, there is no competition to drive up the price. The bidder then either gets a bargain or the piece may even go unsold for failure to meet an undisclosed "reserve," or minimum acceptable, price set by the seller.

For the same reasons that Canadian upper-level antiques prices are typically low by international standards, because of an insufficient demand and buyer base for the finest pieces, Canada is also not an international auction market. Both dealers and branches of auction houses do a great deal of shipping around, trying to find the best locations and venues for sales. Antiques of Canadian origin or of specifically Canadian interest might be returned to Canada as the best venue for sale. They may equally do just as well if sold anywhere else, since Canadian specialist dealers and collectors watch the auction market worldwide.

The reverse is not true. Few American, British, or European buyers watch the Canadian auction market. Thus, for maximum exposure, a collector or auction house here that offers a fine and high-value European, English, or American piece would logically send it to London or New York for sale. Conversely, no collector or auction house, internationally, would even think of sending a potentially half-million or million-dollar piece to Toronto for sale, for the Canadian high-value market is just too small.

Price Standards

One problem of buying or selling in a completely unfettered and fragmented market is the absence of any dependable standards or price track records. Unlike stock, bond, commodity, or real-estate markets, there are no centralized antiques markets or price-recording systems. Prices can vary widely for very similar or even identical objects, depending on where and how they are sold – and to whom. Larger auction houses that publish sale catalogues also publish post-sale price records, but these are usually available only to subscribers to their catalogues. Dealer sales prices are not recorded in any organized way and, like private person-to-person sales, get known only through the market grapevine.

The dealers' associations, which could be in the best position to collect sales figures on both auction and dealer sales, and to maintain continuous databases of sale prices, are of little help. The Professional Art Dealers Association of Canada (PADAC) and the Canadian Antique Dealers Association (CADA) were originally organized to establish ethical and business standards and to police their memberships. Adherence to ethical standards, however, remains largely voluntary. From a self-policing aspect, neither association has any ability to discipline a member, much less to suspend a member from business. Membership is not compulsory, and the great majority of dealers are not members. In fact, anyone can open an art gallery or antiques shop with an ordinary municipal retail business licence. Not even that is needed for private or antiques-show-only dealing. Neither is any special education, knowledge, nor licensing necessary to be a dealer.

In dealers' shops or at antiques shows, similar or identical objects can be offered for very different asking prices at different venues. Pricing seems to be governed by where the shops or antiques shows are located, and what level of potential buyers those dealers and shows appeal to or are trying to attract. Auction prices, too, depend on the level of the auction and the preferences and finances of the bidders who attend.

If you take a Sunday-afternoon foray, with visits to a few village antiques shops or an antiques show, it is easy to see and compare the disparities. In different shops or booths, all offering mainly Definition-3 antiques, common pieces such as 1930s wooden butter boxes, copper water kettles, turned wooden kitchen bowls, or Crown or Beaver canning jars, just as examples, can be priced all over the lot, with common variations of 200 to 400 per cent for exactly the same items.

Just out of curiosity, I recently surveyed this, making notes on some commonly available Definition-3 pieces at a 150-booth antiques show. In that show, among the different dealers, there were nine identical wooden 1930s CANADIAN BUTTER/SASKATCHEWAN boxes, all in similar condition. The asking prices, all within the same show, ranged from $20 to $110. There were also four identical copper water kettles, not overly dented and nicely polished up, all made and marked GSW (General Steel Wares), all from the 1926-to-1932 period. The asking-price spread was $45 to $135. It seems that many dealers determine their asking prices not according to known market values or any standard criteria, but according to what they paid for it, plus pure whim or wish-hope of what they figure the market might bear.

The antiques market, whether in shops or at shows, is anything but a fixed-price market. Asking prices on tags simply reflect dealers' hopes, and starting points for negotiations. No one actually pays the asking price. The real antiques-market scene, though perhaps quieter, is instead more akin to a Middle Eastern bazaar or a Mexican *mercado centrale*. Everything is negotiable. Sellers may drop to nearly their own costs for pieces they have had too long. Buyers may walk away from haggling sessions to return later for another try. Sellers may hold firm, hoping for an easier sale later. Buyers have even been known to play chicken with sellers, slowly and ever more slowly laying out bills in a neat row. Waiting to see who blinks first – the seller accepting the row with its last addition or the buyer suddenly sweeping up his bills – calls for strong nerves. The negotiations and haggling are a large part of the sporting end of antiques buying and collecting.

The Hierarchy

Though it is not often considered or mentioned in relation to the pricing structure of the antiques market, there is very much an unstated hierarchy of dealers and auction houses in Canada, in the customers they appeal to, and in the prices they can command. As with collectors, there are, in effect, two quite distinct antiques markets: the lower-end general and the upmarket specialized. This is probably similar to other marketing businesses, if one considers the spread between, say, Biway and Holt Renfrew in clothing, or Ikea and the Art Shoppe or Ridpath in furniture. In antiques shops, it is a long way from Queen Street East to Davenport Road in Toronto, or in auctions, from rural farm auctions to Sotheby's. In Quebec, the distance from St. Jean port Joli to Sherbrooke Street in Montreal is as great.

At the lower end of the market are the "pickers" as bottom-feeders, buyers who acquire pieces directly from houses or barns and then auction or resell to dealers. Pickers even knock on doors, asking to buy "old stuff" or cast-off "junk." This direct-approach technique is also known as "brushing out" objects that have never previously been in the antiques market. Since much of Canada has by now been picked out for original-source antiques, door-to-door picking is time-inefficient except in a few older and long-settled areas.

Instead, pickers now advertise often by regular classified ads in rural weekly newspapers. A recent and typical ad, under "Wanted to Buy," specified: "Old cupboards, washstands, blanket boxes, oil lamps, fruit jars, crocks, etc. You could have $$ in your attic or basement. Call. . . ." It should be noted that pickers avoid using the word "antique" in their buying, lest it raise sellers' expectations, preferring the term "old."

Toward the top of the hierarchy, a small minority of upmarket and specialized private art and decorative-arts dealers cater to the equally upscale and rarefied-collector customer base that appreciates and can afford their offerings. It is these dealers who can risk buying single $20,000 or even $50,000 objects that no one lower in the hierarchy would dare try. It is likewise the upmarket auction houses that can attract consignments of $100,000-and-up paintings, pictures that country auctioneers or lower-level auction houses could never sell at prices like that.

Because of the hierarchy, there is always a great amount of buying and selling between dealers, probably a much higher volume in fact than of end sales to actual collectors. Dealers do far more of their buying at auctions or from other dealers than from private individuals offering things for sale. From first discoveries and resales by pickers, or sales at country auctions or by small-scale rural dealers, to perhaps ultimate sales at top-dollar by Davenport Road dealers or through Sotheby's, antiques tend to climb a ladder in the market, moving upward from lower-level to larger and better-known upscale dealers or venues. Every antique will eventually reach its optimum price level. Thus, many antiques go around and around within "the trade," at ever increasing prices. They may travel from one antiques show and dealer to another for many months before finally landing with a collector, home-furnisher, or perhaps museum end-buyer, or being retired for a time because of overexposure or overpricing.

Price Guides

The stock price of IBM, General Motors, and thousands of other securities is known every business day, as is the price of many commodities such as wheat, corn, live cattle and hogs, coffee, copper, or oil. With antiques, however, in the absence of any database records or broadspectrum price tracking and quotations, there are only two ways of establishing values and prices. One is to check past auction price records, which may be several years old, for sales of similar objects. Market-oriented antiques papers such as *Antique Showcase, The Upper Canadian*, and *Maine Antique Digest* also often cover auctions and antiques shows, including scattered or representative asking- and sales-price summaries.

There are also probably hundreds of published price guides, some encyclopaedic and all-inclusive, but many of them subject-specialized, for everything from glass or ceramics to tools, postcards, or political memorabilia. These can be compiled from actual sales at antiques shows or auctions, or from hoped-for asking prices. Because the sources are diverse (and rarely cited), the prices listed usually have substantial high-to-low spreads. Since very similar pieces often sell at widely different prices in different places, however, records from past sales or published price guides are at best only a very loose indicator of likely prices in present or future sales.

The other way to establish a price for a specific object, of course, is actually to buy or sell it. The value, at one time and in one place, then becomes the price that is negotiated and agreed upon, or that a piece brings at auction. Even so, that represents the value only of a single piece in a single transaction between a single seller and a single buyer. That price, were it to be published and known, still would set only a loose precedent for whatever price might be negotiated or bid in another sale.

Condition

Physical condition can make a horrendous difference to values and prices. Generally speaking, repaired or restored breakables such as glass, ceramics, or small wooden objects have greatly reduced values, for they can now only be displayed, but are no longer usable. A piece of pottery that has been cracked or broken, no matter how carefully repaired, may be worth half to a quarter of an identical piece that has never been damaged. A glass flask or a mould-blown goblet with a small chip missing from the lip can be worth as little as half the value of an unchipped piece. A piece of furniture "in the rough," or in battered and unrestored condition, may be worth a fifth to a tenth, or even less, of what a dealer might ask for it after restoration.

Buyers generally want their antiques instantly usable or displayable. Few collector-buyers have the skills themselves or want the hassle and cost of restoring pieces in the rough. Thus, a restored piece, ready to go into someone's home, is worth far more than a piece in sorely distressed condition. *Skilled and careful* restoration of such objects as furniture, paintings, rare books, or antique cars can substantially improve the price, with the quality of the restoration making the greatest difference. Poor, botched, or overdone restoration – or worse, heavy and inept faked alteration – will decrease the value, and instead is destructive (Figs. 10, 11).

Let's suppose a dealer picks up a basically good but very in-the-rough pine two-tiered cupboard for $1,200 at a country auction, a piece with perhaps several coats of overpaint and some missing shelves and mouldings. He has paid top dollar for the cupboard in as-is condition. Then he has a good restorer-refinisher, charging perhaps $30 or $40 an hour, spend twenty hours or more stripping, refinishing, and replacing missing parts. The dealer's cost base is now up to around $2,000 or $2,200. Since the cupboard is in saleable condition, the dealer will probably try for a 100-per-cent mark-up and price the cupboard in his shop at $4,500, or maybe even $5,000. Perhaps he can get that or close to it, or maybe not, for the asking price is always negotiable, and most potential buyers will, or should, haggle over the asking price.

The dealer was probably justified in putting $1,000 in restoration costs into a piece for which he paid $1,200 in poor condition, *if* the piece is otherwise good and genuine and he knows he can eventually get something approaching $4,500 or $5,000 for it. Dealers are essentially speculators, betting that they can get more for pieces than they paid for them. Every purchase a dealer makes is a judgement call and a financial risk, and there is always the chance of paying too much for a piece that will not sell very readily. If our dealer eventually takes $4,000, or even just $3,500, for his restored cupboard, he has probably come out smiling.

Perhaps the greatest price differences because of condition can be seen in antique coins. With coins, there are seventy standard condition gradations, with possible value spreads of up to 4,000 per cent for the very same coin (Fig. 3). Thus, determining coin conditions is a nit-picking and hair-splitting affair. Value and price differences because of condition are perhaps not that extreme with most antiques, but still often call for very subjective appraisals and judgements. In the end, however, the real value of any antique as of that moment comes down to an actual sale, a negotiated agreement between buyer and seller, or what the object brings at auction.

Liquidity

Because of the fragmented and unstructured nature of the antiques market, a most important investment consideration is always the question of liquidity. How quickly can one sell something, and at what price? Every antiques-market exposure of an object, whether in a dealer's shop, an antiques show, or a local auction, is necessarily limited. Most antiques auctions or shows do not attract attendance from great distances. Thus, except for widely and expensively publicized country-wide or international auctions, with glossy brochures and colour-filled catalogues, the exposure of a piece and the potential number of buyers or sellers is generally quite localized.

With truly rare and supreme pieces, word of mouth or selective collector targeting, complete with phoning or letter-writing by dealers, spreads the word. Private dealers operate solely by advertising and customer targeting, without the overhead costs of shops or large inventories. In general, however, because of limited exposure, Collector X in Hawaii is not likely to know that Halifax Dealer Y has a piece he might be interested in, or that Collector Z in Toronto is thinking of parting with a few pieces.

What one can expect to net in selling an antique is always chancy. Collectors, would-be collectors, and plain generalist acquirers should always view published price guides and listings, whether in stamp and coin catalogues, in auction sales listings, or in antiques newspaper show reports, as distorted toward the high side. The price listings are invariably of selected retail sales or asking prices before haggling, but they do not really reflect what an owner is actually likely to get for a piece he wants to sell. In all antiques markets, for quick sales some retail dealers even discount their asking prices from those in published catalogues or price guides, while others will try to push the market higher.

The centralized and international stock, bond, or commodities markets, as well as gold and precious metals, are relatively liquid. Even in a declining or plummeting market, one can always sell and still usually manage to cut one's losses and get out of the market within the same day. With quick electronic matching of worldwide buy and sell orders, there is always a buyer, at whatever price.

Selling tangible property such as antiques means that the seller must actually find buyers. In an object-saturated or declining market, however, there may be no buyers, or not enough buyers for the number of pieces appearing on the market. Thus, sellers of art and antiques, much like those selling real estate, can wind up stuck with their assets for a long time, unable to liquidate and get out, except at a substantial loss.

Antiques are simply not as readily disposable at full value as more usual investments. Centralized and computerized stock, bond, and commodity markets, operating internationally and electronically, and with daily price quotations available to anyone who can read a newspaper, can usually match buyers and sellers almost instantly. With antiques, however, one cannot simply call one's broker and buy or sell immediately, much less at a reasonably known price. Again, more like real estate or the used-car business, marketing antiques is wholly a matter of individual negotiations between any buyer and any seller. Selling comes only after offers and counteroffers, and will not necessarily happen quickly.

Aside from their uncertain liquidity, antiques, as all tangible objects, have some other severe downsides as investments. First, antiques in any form are a non-productive, or static, investment. Like gold, diamonds, or other precious metals, they generate no continuous interest or dividend income. Held long enough, and sold at the right time and price, antiques can produce only capital gains, and then only when they are sold.

Antiques and art are also acquired with collectors' after-tax discretionary income, and after most other necessities and cost-of-living expenses. Consequently, antiques collecting, and the whole art and antiques market as an economic entity, really lies on the outer fringes of economic life. Because of that marginal position, art and antiques values and prices are very sensitive and vulnerable to broader economic shocks or downturns. Antiques and art are among the first non-essential possessions to be liquidated – sometimes even dumped at fire-sale prices – in a severe recession, but among the last to be acquired – after houses, new cars or appliances, or after paying off debts – in an economic recovery or upswing.

There are some good examples of this. From the late 1960s to 1973, Japanese investor-speculators discovered French Impressionist paintings and, at auction sales, drove prices out of sight. Then came the 1973 OPEC oil embargo, oil and gasoline shortages, and fuel-price paranoia. The Japanese investor-speculators were suddenly dumping rather than buying, and getting out of the French Impressionist market. With that major buyer base gone, prices at auction dropped by about 30 per cent.

During the 1981–82 recession, particularly, many investor-speculators were badly burned when art and antiques prices all but collapsed. Some pieces at auction then were selling for 25 to 40 per cent less than prices the very same pieces had brought in the mid-1970s. As gold and silver bullion prices escalated in 1980, while antiques prices were falling, the collector value of much antique and "semi-antique" silver and jewellery fell below its metal value. Great quantities were actually melted down. In some Toronto art and antiques auction sales, up to 30 per cent of the lots offered went unsold when they failed to achieve their reserve prices.

The latest example of large-scale art and antiques dumping occurred from 1993 to 1995. A great many Lloyd's insurance investors, or "names," with unlimited liability, were assessed with huge claims to cover syndicate losses from such events as the Exxon Alaskan oil spill, Florida's Hurricane Andrew, the Northridge, California, earthquake, and several other disasters. To cover them, many of these people put art and antiques collections on the market, mostly at auction through venues such as Sotheby's in London, Geneva, and Baden-Baden. Fortunately for the sellers, the quality of these collections was excellent, and economies generally were recovering from the 1989–92 recession. Thus, in spite of the sudden dumping, buyers were there, values held, and the sales even achieved some record prices.

Just as with the short-lived Japanese speculative love affair with French Impressionist paintings, the market values of some categories of Canadian antiques are also very subject to fads and fashions. Generalist collectors, since they are largely decor-oriented, are also more fashion-motivated than are specialists, and what they collect is often more vulnerable to changing shifts in fashion that may affect prices.

Since the late 1970s, later Victorian, "Arts and Crafts," and Edwardian furniture of the period from 1860 to 1914 has come into vogue. Most of that was factory-manufactured furniture, not created by individual cabinetmakers and, until recently, was considered just old used furniture. French-Canadian furniture, usually scalped to bare wood and refinished, was and still is in fashion, and, as mentioned, the most elaborate of Quebec armoires and three-drawer commodes have brought the highest prices of any Canadian furniture. "Folk" art has also come into vogue since the 1940s, including even recent and deliberately created market-oriented folk art (Fig. 9), with its price levels supported only by fashion-generated demand, not by quality or rarity. Fads and fashions, of course, are rarely long-lived or permanent. The prices of faddish antiques, with the ebbing of fashion-driven demand, can easily go down as rapidly as they went up.

Mechanisms of Selling

To sell within a short time, whether you are disposing of a sizeable collection or just grandmother's old rocking chair, it may be necessary to solicit offers from several different dealers. Among antiques dealers, there are all categories and persuasions, from pickers and flea-market purveyors to high-end specialists, all with different markets. Most dealers, and particularly specialists, have known – if not necessarily well-established – customer bases, and their different priorities and market exposures affect what they will buy and what they will pay for something.

All dealers, as all collectors, will try to buy for the least and sell for the most, but many dealers will decline to buy any but the finest or most quickly saleable pieces, unless they expect at minimum to double their money. Thus, if a dealer thought he or she could get perhaps $400 for your grandmother's rather ordinary rocking chair, the dealer would probably offer you no more than $200, or maybe $250 – if it was in saleable condition as-is and he or she thought it might sell quickly.

Beyond that, if the dealer smelled a distress sale, and suspected that you needed money quickly and *had* to sell the rocking chair, he might well seize the chance and offer you as little as $150 or even $100. Though many dealers will be fair with individual sellers, there are always circling vultures. Distressed sellers, whether of stocks and bonds, art and antiques, or real estate, always present fertile opportunities for predacious bargain-hunters.

Antiques dealers must plan on substantial mark-ups. As well as the operational costs of running a shop, dealers often have a high-cost inventory but a low sales volume. The inventory turnover of an antiques shop does not approach that of a supermarket or a hardware store. Pieces can sit for months, even years, tying up the dealer's capital, before a buyer comes along. Thus, every dealer must try to operate on very high margins, since those margins must carry all of the capital and operating costs. Otherwise that dealer is not long in business.

Of the various possible options for selling, selling to a dealer is beyond doubt the quickest, since it brings immediate payment. It is also likely, however, to net the seller the lowest percentage of the optimum value, since the dealer will offer the minimum he or she thinks the seller might accept. The seller who knows what he or she has, and roughly its value, has a distinct advantage, and is in a far better position to negotiate or to refuse unrealistic offers.

If the person wanting to sell something is even loosely knowledgeable about the antiques market, the best route can often be selling directly, through an advertisement in one or more of the antiques papers or magazines mentioned earlier. There is also nothing like phone calls or faxes to a carefully targeted list of potential buyers, including selected dealers. This is particularly true for fine or rare pieces in high demand. The item may not sell immediately, or at the asking price. It probably won't, but the ads or faxes may well bring on negotiations or counteroffers. Direct selling is also the route most likely to net the seller a price closest to real value, minus only the cost of the ads or phone bills.

The auction route, particularly for selling large collections in their entirety or extremely high-value pieces that will generate heavy buyer competition, is usually preferable to selling either to dealers or by the direct route, and is often the only viable option. In looking at a large collection, for example, both dealers and other collectors are always going to want to "cherry-pick." Few collections are composed of equally superlative pieces. Buyers will want to take only the most desirable pieces, but not want the collection as a whole, except at a very low overall price. Dealers do not like taking on whole collections, for while they can readily sell the best, they are likely to remain stuck with the lesser pieces. Auctions will at least sell everything.

Larger auction houses that publish illustrated catalogues can also offer far broader sales exposure than either individual classified ads or dealers' shops. The auction climate, with dozens or perhaps hundreds of people attending, also creates bidding competition that is absent in most private sales. Thus, auctions are the only selling venue where prices are bid up during individual sales, rather than being beaten down as they often are during private negotiations.

The downside of the art and antiques auction route is the time it takes to sell something, the unpredictability of prices, and the sales-cost deductions. An auction house will typically accumulate consignments, from many different sources, for months before a scheduled sale. The luring of seller-consignors, and the assemblage, cataloguing, and advertising of sales, all takes time.

If the auction is a specialized, or "theme," sale, featuring only one or two categories of objects, the lead time to assemble a sale can be up to a year. Theme sales are increasingly popular in the auction business, because they attract and concentrate special-interest and like-minded buyers, which the auctioneers hope will increase bidding competition and, therefore, sale prices. People attending theme sales are likely to be specialists, however, and more discriminating than general auction audiences. Theme-sale audiences are also likely to be dominated by dealers, who are buying for resale. Prices are typically lower, and poor or mediocre pieces often do less well than in general sales.

While the actual prices that objects bring at auction emerge only in the sale, the auction houses, in their catalogues, often publish high and low advance estimates. The estimates, however, are just the auction houses' opinions of what they think various pieces might bring. In actual sales, many pieces sell for less than the low estimate or can go well above the high estimate.

Among the many types of auctions, art and antiques sales are considered to be seller controlled. Sellers can negotiate commissions, set minimum "reserve" prices, or withdraw pieces. Reserve prices, or the lowest amount the seller will accept, are typically about 60 to 80 per cent of the low estimate. The reserve is not disclosed either in the catalogue or on the floor. Only the auctioneer knows. In cases where there is only a single active bidder, the auctioneer may also use the secret reserve price to create the impression of a second bidder. Taking bids "off the wall," he will try to get the bid price at least up to the reserve. This is risky for both the seller and auctioneer, for the sole real bidder may drop out. If bidding fails to meet the reserve, the piece goes unsold, a quite common occurrence that auctioneers try to avoid. Even that is not usually announced, though the auctioneer may hammer as he "buys in" the piece for return to its consignor. After a sale, however, consignors often rethink their reserve price, and after-sale deals on unsold pieces are common.

Depending on the buyers who attend, auctions can also be subject to one-time flukes, with pieces either being severely undervalued or setting price records. Thus, to the seller, consigning something at auction is very much a gamble or, as the Japanese say, auctions are functions of fate.

As an example, I long ago had an ancient aunt in New York who had inherited a nice but not truly fine Massachusetts 1770s-period maple slant-front desk. She couldn't fit it into her apartment and wanted to sell it, and she knew the market reasonably well. She called in one of the biggest dealers in New York, who wanted the desk and offered her $1,200 for it – this in the late 1950s. Though then in her early eighties, Aunt Helen was pretty astute, and told him she wouldn't take a nickel less than $3,000. The dealer upped his offer to $1,500 and finally, reluctantly, to $1,800. Aunt Helen was well fixed and didn't really need the money. She just wanted to part with the desk, but not enough to "give it away," as she put it when telling the story later. A tough old bird, she was. No deal.

She then consigned the desk to Parke Bernet (before its Sotheby's merger), with a $3,000 reserve. Ever determined, she actually attended the auction, sitting in the back row. Then she cheated and bid herself two or three times to boost the price. This was risky, for she could have wound up buying her own desk and paying the commission. Sellers are not supposed to bid on their own pieces, though nothing can really prevent that.

Aunt Helen was a cagey old girl, or maybe just lucky. With two other bidders still going, having made her reserve, she dropped out at the $3,250 bid. The desk finally went for $4,500, and to exactly the same dealer who had earlier told her that $1,800 was his "absolute outside limit." For quickly saleable antiques, dealers will sometimes pay very close to what they hope to get for pieces they really want. Equal knowledge and nerve on the seller's part, however, is essential for dealing with dealers.

Financially, the deductions from the gross sale prices that the auction seller receives are usually more than the costs of selling directly through ads or phoning and faxing around, but usually less than the discounts from optimum value incurred in selling to dealers.

Auction houses once operated on a straight 10-per-cent commission, later raised to 15 per cent, which was deducted from the sale price. No longer. Where dealers will usually at least try to discount 50 per cent for pieces they buy, most auction houses now take a seller's commission of 15 per cent of the gross price, or "hammer" price, that an item brings at sale. A few are even trying for 20-per-cent sellers' commissions, though that may discourage seller-consignors. Many auction houses also now start with a minimum commission of $75 or $100. Thus, with a $75 minimum, unless an item sells for at least $500, the auction-house seller's commission is actually much greater than 15 per cent.

Some years ago the art and antiques auction industry also began charging buyers' commissions, which were introduced by Christie's to great yelling and moaning, but the idea stuck as other auction houses joined in. Buyers' commissions now also run at 10 per cent or sometimes 15 per cent of sales prices. At 15 per cent and 10 per cent respectively from both sellers and buyers, for a piece selling at a "hammer" price of $1,000, the buyer pays $1,100, with the buyer's commission added. The net amount finally paid to the consigning seller by the auction house is then $850, after deduction of the seller's commission. The auction house takes $250.

The consignor's actual payment will, in fact, probably be less. Auction houses will milk sellers as far as they can. Thus, any costs for shipping, for auction-catalogue illustrations, or for insurance coverage will all be deducted from the eventual payment to the consignor, usually about a month after the sale. The auction house then collects, from both ends, a total commission of 25 or 30 per cent, or more for sales of under $500, plus all extra costs. The buyer's commission, plus GST and PST on the item bought, plus GST on the buyer's commission as well, means the auction buyer of the $1,000 antique ultimately winds up paying nearly $1,300 for it.

Therefore, the add-ons of buyers' commissions and taxes effectively add a quarter or more to hammer prices. Since buyers are quite aware of the buyers' commissions and taxes, this clearly depresses bidding and reduces auction prices received. It also provides an advantage to dealers who are trying to buy directly from sellers.

No other form of auctioning, whether of cattle and horses, house contents, or bankruptcy or receivership sales, attempts to levy buyers' commissions, for the sellers know they could not get away with it. Instead, they often deduct higher sellers' commissions than the art and antiques auction houses, typically 20 or 25 per cent.

In private or dealer sales, no matter whether the prices are actual optimum value or not, the price paid and received is the price directly negotiated. Unlike arm's-length auction sales, in direct sales both buyer and seller also have control over the sale and the ultimate price, as well as the sport and pleasure of negotiating eyeball to eyeball, whatever their haggling tactics.

In spite of the commissions and extraction of costs by auction houses, however, the net sale prices finally paid to consignors are still typically more than the discounted prices that can be offered to sellers by dealers. Over the past twenty-five years or so, particularly for selling major or high-demand pieces, or entire large collections, there has been a strong trend away from selling to dealers and toward consigning at auction. This has created rapid growth in the auction industry. As well as the old, established international auction venues such as Christie's, Phillips, or Sotheby's, dozens if not hundreds of more recent regional art and antiques auction houses have come into existence, from Bourne and Skinner in Massachusetts to James Julia in New Hampshire to Joyner, Ritchie's, or Reeve & Mackay in Toronto.

This plethora of auctioning opportunities for sellers has eroded the earlier pre-eminence of dealers as middlemen in the antiques and art markets. It has also introduced real competition among auction houses. To attract truly prime consignments, large collections, and the finest "sale-leader" pieces, auction houses now, though quietly, often negotiate reduced seller commissions and other seller perks.

Fifty years ago the auction market was limited and primarily wholesale, selling very largely to dealers. In recent decades auction houses have massively expanded their advertising, and auctions have become more and more direct markets for collectors as well. To acquire fine or rare pieces, dealers have increasingly been forced to buy at retail auctions, now often bidding in horn-to-horn competition with major collectors who are going for the same fine pieces. Consequently, dealers' margins have been squeezed, and, to maintain top-quality inventories, they are often forced to buy pieces with little additional profit-potential left in them.

Investment

Dealers, auction houses, and the antiques media sometimes push the concept of antiques as an investment, and that what you acquire today is bound to be worth more tomorrow. Probably that is true, *if* you buy exactly the right pieces and keep them long enough and are astute enough to foresee the market distortions of fashion, speculation, or economic recessions. Reading the mainstream financial media, however, often leads one to the opposite impression: that antiques, even over the long term, are a poor investment compared to stocks, bonds, or equity mutual funds. This is also true, in the great majority of cases.

In reality, just as with anything else, object quality and rarity, and solid collector knowledge, is the determining factor. With antiques, this means original quality and top condition. Was an antique, in its own day, just an ordinary object in daily use that has become antique only with time, or was it originally something special or a superlative piece of craftsmanship in its own right, treasured down through the generations? In antiques, as with milk, the cream always rises to the top. Original high quality in early silver, furniture, or whatever, typically equals present-day scarcity or rarity. It is high quality and rarity together, as well as condition, that then create collector demand.

In terms of values, for investment purposes probably 95 per cent of age-defined antiques may just barely keep up with cumulative inflation, but are unlikely ever to accrue real capital gains. With Definition-3 antiques particularly, as obsolete manufactured objects or "collectibles," there are constantly more pieces on the antiques market than there are collectors or other end-buyers to absorb them. Manufactured objects today also continue to become obsolete and "antique" with great rapidity. Thus, future values of Definition-3 antiques may not even keep up with low inflation, and have no chance of making real (after-inflation, after-tax) capital gains. Historically, the best long-term investments have always been the finest and rarest pieces, and that has been true pretty well across the entire spectrum of antiques categories, from ceramics to furniture to rare books.

For example, the labelled Thomas Nisbet mahogany table mentioned earlier (Figs. 5, 5a), selling today at $20,000, may well be worth $30,000 to $40,000, or perhaps even more, ten years from now. The potential buyer base at that price level may be only a handful of collectors or museums. Because labelled Nisbet pieces are fine and elegant as well as rare, however, there are still far more potential buyers than there ever is Nisbet furniture available (almost never), and always will be. Demand for the finest and rarest antiques is likely to remain continuous – a considerable advantage, for they are not subject to the comings and goings of fashion or home-decorating tastes.

On the other hand, a simple pine country table, selling for under

$500 (Fig. 4), will very likely still be worth about that same price or perhaps a bit more ten years from now. The potential buyer base may be large, perhaps thousands of people, but in endless variation there are also thousands of plain nineteenth-century pine country tables available. Every other antiques shop seems to have at least one, so at any particular time there are probably more plain pine tables – even genuine antique ones – for sale than there ever are immediate buyers. As the most common form of reproduction, new pine tables are also being turned out by the thousands, just adding to the oversupply. Thus, the price values of plain pine tables are relatively static and are likely to remain that way.

The same situation applies to a great many other categories of antiques, where the quantities available seem to match or even exceed immediate demand. This is what is called "economic equilibrium," where supply and demand are roughly equal. Values and prices then remain fairly stable or advance only slowly for a very long time, offering little chance for any real capital gain.

In the overall economy, cumulative inflation in Canada over the last thirty years has been roughly 600 to 700 per cent. In purchasing power, although there are lots of exceptions, that means on average that a $10 item in the 1960s now costs approximately $60 to $70 (plus sales taxes). How many antiques, of Canadian or any origin, have appreciated 600 to 700 per cent in value over the past thirty years, just keeping even with cumulative inflation? The answer is only a minority, and that minority has been limited to the very best and most desirable antiques in a totally open market.

Pulling It Together

It seems pretty clear that the best way to have even a reasonable chance of financial success in antiques collecting is to stick to collecting the finest and rarest. As outlined earlier, liquidation and selling of art and antiques may be, at best, uncertain and slow. Predicting prices is also very uncertain. Antiques are static and non-income-producing investments and do not have the immediate or quick disposal potential of more conventional investment forms. With dealers' own purchases from sellers heavily discounted to provide them with the necessary high retail margins, or with auction houses' heavy commissions, the selling costs in disposing of art or antiques are also far higher than for any other investment form, including stocks, bonds, commodities, or real estate.

High sales costs mean that an individual selling any antique, *just to barely break even*, has got to have an estimated value of original cost, *plus* cumulative inflation, *plus* a capital gain of at least 20 to 25 per cent over that cost-plus-inflation total if going to auction, or up to 50 per cent if selling to a dealer. Very few antiques achieve that level of appreciation.

So, if you like early Canadian country pine and maple furniture, or simple redware and stoneware pottery, nineteenth-century glass bottles, or early carpenters' tools, you should be collecting for just that reason, because you enjoy having them and have an emotional attachment and feel for the culture and history that they represent. They should be collected for the aesthetic or historical pleasure and satisfaction they give you, but not primarily as a money-making investment.

For that 90-plus per cent of antiques in the market today that fall into Definition-3, as obsolete objects, but lack the ingredients either of special quality or rarity, forget ideas of substantial capital gain. Opportunity for real capital gain, short-term or long-term, after the erosion of inflation and after eventual sales costs and taxes, simply is not there. Thus, there is no real investment potential.

For collecting that actually may have real investment and capital-gain potential, the combination of *all* of age, quality, rarity, and condition is essential. Rarity alone does not necessarily indicate quality, but scarcity or rarity combined with collector demand is certainly the strongest single determiner of value. If any one of the four elements is lacking, however, investment potential is reduced or simply absent. As they say in real estate, the key to value is "location, location, location." In antiques, it is "quality, rarity, condition," also repeated three times. Thus, any collector-investor who entertains hopes of eventual real capital gain has little choice but to stick to acquiring the finest.

A retired and now-deceased successful private dealer once gave me the finest piece of capsule advice I have yet heard on antiques as an investment. "Go after what buyers are competing with each other to buy," he told me. "Forget about what sellers are competing to sell." He was, of course, quite right. Selling competition stabilizes or even reduces prices, particularly when a lot of material is available. Instead, it is buyer competition for the finer and scarcer objects that steadily pushes up prices and ultimately creates capital gains.

In this attempt to outline the economics of the Canadian antiques market, I am not going to get into offering antiques investment advice or recommend any particular collecting categories or choices as good or bad investments. That is an individual decision. Personal knowledge, a sharp eye and mind, and deliberate, careful judgement is, of course, essential. Any collector should visit museums at every opportunity, to observe, absorb, and learn. Any collector, in what amounts to a continuous learning process, should also be buying at least one book for every object that he or she acquires.

Continual learning is an absolute prerequisite to successful buying or collecting. In the realm of antiquaries, there really are no "experts," only aging students. In the jungle and the grand game that is the antiques market – full of gems, treasures, and occasional "sleepers," as well as traps, thorns, and creatures that bite – continuous study, knowledge, experience, judgement, and caution are the best defences a collector has.

Caveat emptor.

2

Scams and Scammers:
Who Does What to Whom

———◆◆◆◆◆———

"There's a sucker born every minute."

— Phineas Taylor Barnum, 1852

A story goes around of a wealthy New York art collector bargain-hunting a few years ago among the myriad small antiques shops that dot rural Quebec. In a roadside shop that was really a packed-full barn, south of Quebec City, the dealer invited him to rummage around out in back. From under the seat of a dilapidated horse-drawn sleigh, the collector pulled a little painting, covered with what seemed to be years of dust and dirt.

Blowing off some of the dust, and looking at the painting even in the gloom of the barn, the collector was delighted. He recognized it as a portrait of a nineteenth-century habitant, painted, he was sure, in the 1850s by the famous Quebec artist Cornelius Krieghoff. Brushing the surface with his sleeve, he could even make out a bit of the artist's signature. He took the painting to the front of the barn. The dealer took one glance and said, "That's a good Krieghoff. Had it for years now. Just a little dirty. Got a lot in it, so I've got to ask five thousand for it."

The collector didn't even quibble. He quickly hauled out a thick wad of cash and counted out fifty hundred-dollar bills. "My God," he thought, "what a steal! These country dealers are way behind the real world. This picture would bring twenty or thirty thousand at a Toronto or New York art auction."

Then he wondered. He knew about Canada's cultural-property export law, and had himself experienced a spot of trouble in Italy and Greece. Would he be trying to smuggle a national treasure back to New York? Worse, might he get caught?

"Not to worry," said the dealer. "Take it to my brother François, about a kilometre up the road. He's an artist with a studio, and he can fix it for you, no problem."

François took a look, and sprayed the still-dusty Krieghoff with a neutral fixative. He then overpainted the Krieghoff *habitant* with a portrait of then-premier Jacques Parizeau, which he copied from a photograph on the front page of the morning's newspaper.

Safely back in New York, with no Canadian export problem, the collector took the picture to his restorer and explained the overpainted portrait. "No problem," said the restorer, and set to work.

Off came the overpainted portrait of Jacques Parizeau. Next, off came the Krieghoff portrait of the habitant. Finally, from underneath those covering paint layers emerged another and original portrait of Jacques Parizeau.

That sad tale is just an illustration of the incidence of fakery in Canadian antiques that has spread over the last forty years, and particularly since the 1967 Centennial of Confederation.

Fakery has been going on ever since collecting began. The human animal is very acquisitive, like ravens and pack rats. Any object that possibly can be collected *is* collected, by someone somewhere, from elegant works of art to bar matchbooks and swizzle sticks. Thus, collecting, followed quickly by faking, is probably as ancient an activity as beer-brewing or prostitution. In Europe, certainly, identified faking of antiquities has been going on at least ever since wealthy ancient Roman collectors created a demand for even-more-ancient classical Greek statuary, and probably much earlier. There is some archaeological evidence that even early cave-dwellers may have collected different types of flint knives and spear-points.

Fakery – of paintings, silver, furniture, or anything else – in most cases is a purely economic activity, aimed solely at creating or improving value. Fakery good enough to pass critical judgement also requires great skill and time. As artists and craftsmen, truly superb and successful fakers are every bit as talented and proficient as the best original makers. Fortunately, however, very few fakers are that good.

Faking of antiques, or the selling of fakes, is not an absolute black and white activity. There are many opinions even on the definition of a fake, as well as many degrees and forms of fakery. Thus, the whole issue is full of grey areas, not least the shadowy dividing line between fakes and reproductions. For example, many furniture companies now produce eighteenth-century reproduction furniture, from the Kittinger Company in Buffalo at the high end, licensed to produce very meticulous and expensive Colonial Williamsburg reproductions, to the Bombay Company, advertising low-cost pseudo-Georgian-style reproductions made largely of particle-board and tissue-thin veneer. Then there is a question of where carefully crafted and authentic "museum" reproductions stand. For that matter, is a counterfeit $20 bill a fake or a reproduction – or both?

In Europe, the faking of sculpture, furniture, painting, precious metals and ivory, religious icons, and documents goes back many centuries. The excellence and antiquity of many early and even ancient fakes and forgeries often makes detection difficult or, if one is to be absolutely certain, even impossible. Experts can also make mistakes, and expert opinions can and do sometimes contradict other expert opinions.

Over the past few centuries, many finely crafted objects have been discovered and denounced as fakes. No doubt many other fakes, long in museum or private collections, have never been identified as such. Conversely, many pieces that have previously been declared as fakes, on some earlier expert's opinion, may ultimately turn out to be quite genuine with increasingly sophisticated techniques of testing and analysis.

Though North American collectors of European or Asian antiquities must always be concerned with fakes that are centuries old or even ancient, that is not generally a problem with North American antiques. Since European permanent settlement began only in the early seventeenth century, there are no earlier European-derived objects – simply because no one was here to produce them. Faking is also a particular latecomer to the area of Canadian art and antiques, though it has been current in the United States for over a century and in Britain and Europe for far longer. The reason for this seems twofold.

First, Canada was many decades behind Britain or the United States in coming to any appreciation at all of what might broadly be called material heritage. That term could cover everything from historic architecture and buildings to antique furniture, ceramics, or glass. As recently as the 1950s, early buildings in Canada were being abandoned or demolished, with no thought of restoration or attempts to find optional contemporary uses. Even today, laws protecting historical buildings are quite weak and loose.

Before the Second World War, the Canadian level of awareness and appreciation of material heritage was so low that antique furniture was typically considered as just old and battered – junk. At least as late as the 1930s, old furniture was often simply thrown away or burned, deliberately destroyed. Few people cared. By way of illustration, before 1967 and the government-sponsored wave of national awareness that came with the Centennial, fewer than a dozen books had ever been published on Canadian antiques or historic architecture. There are now several hundred.

Certainly a vast amount of superb Canadian furniture and furnishings, made in the eighteenth and early-nineteenth centuries by skilled individual craftsmen, also disappeared in disastrous fires, particularly the "Great Fires" that periodically ravaged parts of every Canadian city. In the days of fireplace heating and cooking and shaggily mortared chimneys, rural houses and all their contents also burned with great regularity.

Thus, of all the furniture, silverware, glass, or pottery that was either imported or made in Canada before, say, 1850, probably not more than

5 or 10 per cent now survives. Looking at that huge attrition in another way, probably 90 or 95 per cent of the Canadian-made antiques seen in most shops or at antiques shows were made later than 1850. Many shops now offer little or nothing much predating 1900. The survival percentage of pre-1850 buildings, of course, is equally small, if not smaller.

Another reason for the late emergence of fakery in Canada has to do with the nature of the antiques market. While there are at least several thousand antiques dealers across the country, of all levels and persuasions, the market is basically unsophisticated, with a great many decor- and fashion-oriented generalist collectors but relatively few knowledgeable or specialist collectors or dealers.

For that reason alone, fakery in Canadian antiques is largely aimed, its creators and purveyors at least hope, toward the small upper-financial level of the market. Thus, most fakery has been confined to reasonably high-value or potentially high-value objects. There is little point, after all, in a faker investing great time and care to fake most objects, unless genuine versions are of fairly high value as well. If the market value of a plain pine country table did not justify the time, effort, and skill needed to make a fake, then, quite simply, no one would bother faking that sort of table. High demand, however, combined with technically easy and low-cost fakery make pine "harvest" tables not only the most common, but also the most commonly faked or made-up pieces on the present market.

On a purely economic basis, then, if any fake required so much care and time that it would have to sell for as much or even more than a similar genuine piece to offer the faker a good return, it would not be worth the trouble. On that basis, many forms of Canadian antiques on the market, such as elaborately carved and inlaid Victorian furniture, are effectively unfakeable for economic reasons.

Fakers seem to come in two categories: amateurs and professionals. The amateurs appear to be people of indeterminate talent who decide to try something and, judging from results, as often as not make a mess of it. Their products are typically too inept to pass any kind of critical appraisal, though they still get into the antiques market with great regularity.

The professionals, quite the opposite, are usually well trained and experienced in a particular craft. They typically make their living at some more legitimate aspect of their craft, with fakery just an interesting sideline. Professionals are also specialized fakers. Art fakers are artists in their own right, who stick to faking art. Successful furniture fakers are usually fine cabinetmakers, and may even be in the elevated league of marquetry artists or musical-instrument makers. Good silver fakers may be fine jewellers, dental technicians, or silver craftsmen. Successful fakers, overall, know exactly what they are doing, and how to do it, and have the skill and experience to carry it off.

The upper-end players in the antiques market, and its specialist dealers and collectors, are typically the most knowledgeable and experienced, and the most likely to have extensive libraries on the subjects they deal in or collect. While the best fakes may be aimed at the upper-level and higher-value market of specialist collectors, those same specialist dealers and collectors are also in the best position to spot the fakes. In a continual contest between experts, fakery aimed at the specialist market has to be virtually perfect, or at least as undetectable as possible, to have any chance of success.

Because the specialist dealers and collectors make up such a small market in Canada, fakes in this country – or altered and upgraded antiques – are also directed at the financially more upscale market of generalist decor-oriented collectors. The fakery aimed at that market does not have to be thorough or perfect, for that larger market is typically less knowledgeable and experienced and, particularly, far less likely than specialists to examine objects minutely or ask rigorous questions. It is a ripe market for fakers.

Presently, fakery in Canadian antiques is limited to far fewer forms than it is in Europe, again because of the economic limitations. First, of course, come wholly created fakes of entirely new work. Wholly new fakes are extremely uncommon in Canada, except for a very few object types where the making of wholly created fakes is relatively easy. Fakes are never made of pieces that have complex designs, fabrication techniques, or elaborate carving. These would be too difficult and time-consuming to make, and even more difficult to pass off successfully as genuine pieces.

Early and original construction and finishing techniques are very difficult to copy precisely if they are still to appear as original. The patina of age, with wood particularly, is all but impossible to reproduce. Except for some reproduction paint mixtures, the appearance of original finishes now a century or two old can at best be closely approximated, but not really duplicated. What faker is going to spend perhaps some hundreds of hours trying, and very likely failing, to produce a credible piece that would actually pass the close scrutiny of a potential buyer in the $10,000-and-up range? Thus, wholly created fakes are limited to a few subjects, such as Indian trade silver, Quebec chanticleer weathervanes, twentieth-century "folk art," or furniture married or made-up from mixed components of genuine pieces, all areas where relatively high values can be achieved from relatively simple work.

Partial fakery of otherwise early and genuine Canadian antique furniture is by far the most prevalent form in Canadian antiques. The difficulties and time-investment of making, and passing, new and wholly constructed fakes illustrates why the vast majority of Canadian fakes instead take the form of added embellishment or "upgrading," sometimes called "improvement," of existing genuine antique pieces, rather than the creation of wholly new fakes. The result, much more easily accomplished than extensive "antiquing" of brand-new fakes, also remains at least partially genuine (Figs. 6, 7, 7a).

Phineas Taylor Barnum (1810–1891), the famous American showman and huckster, in 1856 gave a speech on that delicious nineteenth-century term "humbug," meaning a hoax, fake, or fraud. Barnum held, quite correctly, that "no humbug is great without truth at the bottom," and that the meaning of humbug was "to take an old truth and put it in an attractive form." As a lifelong master of "humbug," Barnum almost perfectly described upgrading and alteration fakery, all of which is at least based on genuine pieces.

So-called "married" pieces are a blending of parts of two or more original objects, each of which have sections missing, to make a whole piece. This is done particularly – though hardly only – with furniture. Parts of furniture, such as desk-bookcases (Figs. 14, 14a), cupboards in two sections, or Quebec two-tiered buffets (Fig. 17), have often become separated over the years. Dealers will occasionally find a desk base with the upper section missing, or the upper section of a two-tiered buffet with its base section missing. Often that separated, or "divorced," desk base will have its top reworked or replaced, to appear as an original free-standing desk. The buffet upper section will have a new base and legs added, to become a divorced, small, single-unit shallow armoire.

Sometimes, however, rather than create free-standing separate pieces, the faker may do the opposite and blend two unrelated sections into a married composite piece. A dealer may have in storage or manage to acquire both base and upper sections, which, though they don't match and are from different original pieces, with some work are still potentially compatible. Then it becomes the task of a cabinetmaker-restorer, usually working for a dealer, to marry the two into a passable and saleable two-sectioned piece.

With many types of antiques, relatively small details or decorations can also make sizeable differences in the values of pieces otherwise similar or identical, in a price ratio of sometimes ten or fifteen to one. This provides a great window of opportunity for fakers. A plain, anonymous, and unmarked silver church chalice of uncertain origin, though perfectly early and genuine, would be worth perhaps a tenth of exactly the same piece with the punch-marks of a famous French-Canadian silversmith such as Laurent Amiot or François Ranvoyze. A nice but plain round-legged mahogany New Brunswick drop-leaf table, though of the same basic style, form, and age, might be worth roughly one-fifteenth the value of the illustrated Thomas Nisbet piece (Figs. 5, 5a), with its carved and rope-twist legs and maker's label.

Thus, fakers have a strong motivation to add markings (Figs. 20, 46), to apply or improve decorative details (Figs. 8a, 10, 11, 17, 18, 23, 24), or to alter the form or style (Figs. 6, 7, 11) of originally plainer pieces, in the interest of adding value.

A faker, of course, can never get the optimum or highest potential price for his creations. If the potential value improvement, however, might ultimately be 500 per cent, and a faker after some simple work can get just twice what he has invested in a piece in time and cost, then his profit is roughly the same as a dealer's and he has done not badly. If his fakery is competent, the piece will rise further in value as it travels through the antiques market.

"Provenance," or the history of origin, location, and past ownership of an antique, can have a substantial bearing on its value and on determining whether the piece is a fake or reproduction. A piece that is known as once having been owned by a famous person, or that is clearly attributable – though unmarked – to a famous maker, is very likely to be worth more than a piece with no known history.

Provenance is also an indicator of whether an object is genuine. A Canadian piece that has been owned by the same person or has stayed in the same family for at least the past forty or fifty years is unlikely to have been faked. A piece that has remained for several generations in the family of its original owner, and whose maker and place of origin are still known, has the best possible provenance, though that is now relatively rare.

Provenances usually just add to or support basic value, but sometimes values (I should say prices) are almost wholly provenance-based. Good examples of this have occurred particularly with auction sales of movie- and music-star memorabilia, or the chattels of other celebrities. The most extreme example – the feeding frenzy that surrounded the Jackie Kennedy Onassis auction in April 1996 – saw many pieces sell for anywhere from triple to over a hundred times Sotheby's high estimates – based solely on provenance.

Provenances in the antiques market, however, can be easily embellished or even wholly invented. Everyone from little old grandmothers to imaginative dealers can conjure up stories to go with

Fig. 6: Dealers are probably the single greatest source of additions and adulterations to Canadian furniture. To appeal to a largely decor-oriented clientele, many dealers will "improve," or "upgrade," pieces of furniture that were originally simpler into more elaborate pieces. Upgrading is the most common form of fakery.

This mahogany-veneered Nova Scotia bow-front chest of about 1830 is of a desirable small size. In its original form it showed the austerity of most early Nova Scotia furniture – a straight, horizontal lower skirt, plain lathe-turned round front legs, and turned wooden drawer knobs. The present scalloped skirt, Hepplewhite "French" legs, and reproduction brass knobs were all added in a dealer's upgrading of the piece, and are quite well done. The result makes the chest appear twenty years earlier than it actually is, more stylized and formal, and, of course, worth more as an antique than was the simpler original version.

Many dealer alterations and upgradings fall into a grey area of fakery. On this piece, there has been no real attempt to deceive the buyer, except externally and superficially for greater sale appeal. The added new base would be obvious to anyone who turned this piece upside down, as are the modern reproduction knobs.

Fakes or upgradings, a few of which have come into many museum collections over the years, are now considered a very valuable resource. Many museums also have a teaching role, and how better to illustrate fakery and upgrading than with live examples. *Royal Ontario Museum*

Figs. 7, 7a: Another good example of upgrading or add-on fakery, this mahogany-cased tall clock (left) is by W. and G. Hutchinson of Saint John, New Brunswick. The case is reliably attributed to Thomas Nisbet. With its rope-twist quarter-round columns and angled top cornice, the case follows the Empire style of the early 1830s, which dates the clock. The clock and the basic case are quite genuine.

The oval inlay in the pendulum-case door and the broken-arch pediment above the cornice are in a generic Chippendale style of the 1780s and 1790s. Both, however, are stylistically quite wrong for this clock, and are recent upgrading add-ons, as are the small bun feet. As Thomas Hoving wrote in *False Impressions* (1996), "Whether classical, medieval, or modern, such wandering styles suggest a pastiche," which is always suspicious. In this clock, the added oval door inlay is even slightly tipped toward the upper left and lower right, work Thomas Nisbet would never have countenanced.

The nearly identical second clock (Fig. 7a, right) illustrates an original version, never subjected to upgrading. Also by W. and G. Hutchinson, with a Nisbet-attributed case, this clock has the same Empire quarter-columns and cornice as Figure 7, but lacks the recently added pediment, door inlay, or feet. *7 – National Gallery of Canada; 7a – York–Sunbury Historical Museum* their pieces, particularly if they are trying to sell them. The great majority of antiques have long since left their original owners or areas of origin, and their genuine provenances are now unrecorded and unknown.

Family stories can also go well beyond reasonable fiction. Provenances often grow with repetition over the generations, and people have a strong tendency to believe what they want to believe. I am astounded at the amount of inherited 1900s-period English table china from Eaton's that great-grandmother's descendants are certain (or want to believe) came on early-1800s immigrant vessels. I have also seen "Arts and Crafts" period oak factory-made furniture, which stylistically could only have come from a 1900s-period furniture store or mail-order catalogue, that the owners were thoroughly convinced had arrived with Loyalist ancestors.

One day an elderly brother and sister, both in their late seventies, brought me a rust-pitted axe head, and from its shape I could tell it dated from no earlier than perhaps about 1890 to 1920. They were having a sibling spat, and wanted me to give them an opinion on its age and origin. The brother had found the axe head decades ago in a field on his "century" farm, which he said their great-great-grandfather had first started clearing and farming about 1810. He knew, just knew, that it had to be "great-great-grandfather John's pioneer axe." "No," said his sister, whom I suspect was thinking of possible value. "It's a lot older. It's got to be from those French fur traders around here, way back in the old days."

It turned out that their sibling spat about the axe head had been going on for fifty years, and now they expected me to sort it out. Nothing I could say would make them both happy, so I told them it was just an early-twentieth-century axe someone had lost. Who lost it, no one could know, but it was certainly not French fur traders or great-great-grandfather John. They finally went away, thinking I didn't know carrots from apples, still bickering and both still absolutely convinced of his and her chosen provenance for the axe head.

"Attributions" are quite different from provenances. Attributions are experts' opinions or best guesses as to the probable original artists or makers of objects and/or their geographical origins. These opinions are *supposed* to be based on evidence, and on examinations and comparisons with other known work by the same artists or makers or from the same regions. Attributions, however, remain opinions or best guesses, and do not necessarily represent fact or certainty. Since good solid opinions about place of origin or maker attribution are not possible in the majority of cases, provenances are also not usually known.

In Canada, attributions are usually limited to places – provinces, counties, or possibly cities – and to dates of origin, but only occasionally can attributions be made to specific makers. Considering the mobility of people and goods over the last two centuries, broad regional- or provincial-origin attributions are usually the closest best guesses that anyone can reasonably determine.

In practice and in the antiques market, attributions are just as subject to exaggeration or invention as are provenances. The reliability or value of any attribution is only as good as the expertise of whoever rendered the opinion, and the evidence and comparisons on which the attribution is based. In any case, particularly where an attribution is offered by a seller to justify a high asking price, it should be in writing, by a recognized authority, and cite the *reasons* and the *evidence* for the attribution. A solely verbal attribution, and especially one just repeated by someone other than the actual attributor, is just as questionable as a verbal provenance.

I will never forget the shock I got at an antiques show many years ago on meeting a fake attribution that had supposedly been made by me. A dealer had a fairly new and recently imported small crock of German Rhenish salt-glazed stoneware. Rhenish reproduction stoneware has flooded the North American market, but it is easy to spot, even across a room. Unlike most nineteenth-century North American stoneware, the German reproductions are a very even light grey in colour, with no discolourations from firing-temperature variations. They are also not marked. As another clear difference, early North American stoneware after about 1810 always had an interior lining of brown slip, while German stoneware, early or recent, is salt-glazed inside and out.

This Rhenish reproduction had a taped-on tag that, in glowing and flowery terms, announced it was from the Brantford Pottery of Brantford, Ontario, made during Franklin Goold's ownership (1860–1867). The stiff asking price matched the glow of the attribution. The tag also stated that the crock had been "fully examined" and "completely authenticated" by none other than Donald Webster of the Royal Ontario Museum, author of etc., etc. I picked up the piece and turned it over. Sure enough, on the base someone had printed "F. P. Goold" over "Brantford, C.W." in indelible ink. Genuine Canadian stoneware makers' marks were stamped with printer's type, impressed into the wet clay below the pottery rims (Fig. 8).

I conferred with my wife, for this was the sort of situation that is tough to do anything about, barring a loud scene. She decided to have some fun and string things along a little. The woman dealer saw our interest in the crock and came over.

"Do you know Donald Webster?" my wife asked.

"Oh, yes, very well. He's 'authenticated' quite a few of my pieces," the middle-aged dealer responded. I had no idea of how long, or at how many shows, the tag making me look absolutely foolish had been on that German crock.

"And when did he look at this crock?" my wife inquired.

"Oh, I took it to him a couple of months ago," the woman gushed. "He told me it was identical to some shards from their Brantford Pottery [archaeological] dig! He even showed me some!" (My Brantford Pottery dig report had been published several years before, and we'd been in England two months before.)

"If I was interested in your crock, could I double-check it with Mr. Webster, too?" my wife continued.

"Oh, I'm sure he'd be more than willing," the dealer said. "But really, why bother? I'm *sure* he'd tell you the same thing he told me!" I was standing right there, totally unrecognized.

"I think I might have him look at it, anyway," my wife said. "He's here at the show. But first, let me introduce you to my husband."

Fig. 8: David Flack and Isaac Van Arsdale, after 1869, owned a stoneware pottery at Cornwall, Ontario. Many of their pieces, most of which were marked with their name stamped in wet clay, had a distinctive blue decoration of a bird with a scrolled wing top, sitting on a double-scrolled branch. The decorations were done very quickly, by an experienced hand, in sweeping, confident strokes. The blue decorations on all later-nineteenth-century stoneware, Canadian or American, were also invariably on the fronts of the crocks or jugs. Bird-decorated stoneware of this type now sells in the range of $500 to $800. *Private collection*

Fig. 8a: This stoneware jug is an attempt to fake a Flack and Van Arsdale scrolled-bird decoration (Fig. 8). The jug itself is a perfectly genuine later-nineteenth-century piece, though originally unmarked and undecorated, at best a $50 item. The bird is in cobalt-blue glaze, and the jug was actually refired in a kiln to fuse the glaze. The faking is quite obvious. First, the bird is on the side rather than front of the jug, which is never seen on an original piece. Then the decoration was done in slow and hesitant strokes, as if this were the decorator's first attempt – which it probably was. Like 90 per cent of added embellishment or upgrading fakery, this one is readily spotted. *Private collection*

"Oh, I'd be delighted!" the dealer chortled.

"Meet my husband, Donald Webster."

The poor woman turned so pale that I thought she was going to have a cardiac arrest right on the spot. She couldn't talk; she couldn't even stammer. My wife pulled off the tag taped to the crock and put it in her purse, saying that she was "seizing the evidence." Then I told the dealer that not only had I never met her or her falsely attributed crock before, but hoped I never would again. I never wanted to see or hear of her using my name for any reason, ever. I was going to mention this one around, I assured her, and some friends would be watching her pretty closely from then on. I'd be getting reports. We saw her at a distance at a couple of other antiques shows that same year, but never again after that.

Verbal attributions are often casually tossed about or, as with the German crock, quite commonly appear on dealers' description labels or tags. Many are wish-hope guesses, and at best considerably stretch whatever – if any – evidence there might be.

I have also seen photocopies of a few written attributions, bearing letterheads and unfamiliar signatures (supposedly of recognized experts) that were so clearly off base they were certainly forged, simply creative photocopying. The attributions were being used to justify the very high prices of the pieces offered for sale. Naturally enough, the attributions could not be double-checked, for in each case the supposed attributors were conveniently deceased. Unfortunately, I have found that potential buyers rarely attempt to check verbal provenances, attributions, or other background stories. None should ever be taken at face value unless it makes complete sense and, preferably, is documented and reasonably verifiable. As an example, an American art gallery some time ago offered a mid-1940s painting of 1830s Fredericton, New Brunswick (Fig. 9), by the American "folk" painter Grandma Moses (1860–1961). The picture was quite genuine, but the asking price was horrendous. With it was a note, purportedly in Grandma Moses's hand, claiming that the painting was based on stories and descriptions she heard long ago from her father. Hardly! Regardless of the note, the painting was clearly copied and adapted by Grandma

Moses from a well-known and many-times-illustrated 1834 print of Fredericton, entitled the "New Brunswick Fashionables" (Fig. 9a).

Anyone can invent a provenance or attribution or interesting story. If a good but only verbal background is what seems to support or even improve the value and price of an antique, it is always open to question. Whether the background is just the owner's self-delusion, as with most supposed Loyalist pieces, or total fiction, provenance and attribution can be, and all too often are, just as fake as if the object had been faked. Stories should always conform to the probable origins and datings of the antiques. No story is ever any better than the antique itself.

The huge value differences that small details can make explains why the great majority of fakery, in Canadian furniture particularly, takes the form of alteration or upgrading. Much of this involves the addition of embellishments to otherwise simple but basically quite genuine pieces. The majority of this upgrading originates with dealers, who are hoping to improve the value. The upgrading can be just heavy over-restoration and refinishing or can go well beyond that to include substantial changes from original designs or construction (Figs. 6, 7, 11). Some dealers, in refinishing, or "tarting up," persist in trying to make one-hundred- or two-hundred-year-old pieces look like reproductions fresh out of the factory. Depending on their primary market, some dealers also feel that "improvements" are called for, which leads to fake upgrading and alteration (Figs. 6–8, 10–12, 14, 15–18, 22–24, 46).

Some of this alteration and refinishing is well done, making pieces at least superficially seem more stylized, elaborate, or decorative than they originally were (Figs. 6, 7). To generalist collectors, or those interested in decor and fashion, who are not usually purists about originality, this upgrading makes pieces more attractive to contemporary tastes and buyers, and thus more saleable at higher prices by dealers. Dealers are practising the old Chinese adage, that the past must serve the purposes of the present.

Unfortunately, many such embellishments have also been attempted by thoroughly incompetent fakers who should never have been let

Figs. 9, 9a: Since "primitive," or "folk," art has been in fashion ever since the Second World War, most modern folk art is not so much personal expression as it is market-oriented. A contemporary folk artist really ceases to be folk as soon as he or she is discovered (or successfully self-promotes) and becomes commercial. In the realm of paintings, as with woodcarving, much early and modern folk art is derived or copied from something else. Primitive, otherwise untrained, nineteenth-century artists often copied from prints or book illustrations, and some still do. Perhaps 50 per cent of nineteenth- and early-twentieth-century folk paintings that appear today are that sort of copy.

American folk artist Grandma Moses (1860–1961) did this painting (above) of Fredericton, New Brunswick, in 1946, supposedly based on childhood memories of stories and descriptions related by her father. In fact, the painting, with adaptations, is based on and copied after an early lithograph by J. W. Giles, titled the "New Brunswick Fashionables," published in 1834 (Fig. 9a, opposite page). The lithograph has been reproduced and illustrated many times, and would have been easily available to Grandma Moses for copying. *9 – Adamson–Duvannes Gallery, Los Angeles; 9a – Royal Ontario Museum*

NEW BRUNSWICK FASHIONABLES!!!
Fredericton Jan.ᵗʰ 1834.

loose near a piece of wood with a sharp tool (Figs. 10, 10a). Numerous pieces of otherwise quite genuine if simple early furniture have effectively been destroyed by incompetent upgrading, thus losing rather than gaining value.

The greater part of fakery in Canadian antiques seems either poorly or crudely done or it misses some important element. Many fakers seem to concentrate solely on their embellishments, neglecting critical stylistic, technical, or historical considerations, or even simple aesthetics. More fakery probably fails because something just doesn't look right – just smells "wrong" – than for any other reason.

The fake Flack and Van Arsdale stoneware bird jug (Fig. 8a) is a perfect example of an inept faker who went to considerable trouble, including even refiring, to produce a quite incompetent result that shouldn't have fooled anyone, but did. The armoire (Fig. 10, 10a) was attacked by a faker who lavished many hours, perhaps days, carving the intricate floral medallions, but the end result was not just incompetent work, but sheer destruction. Even given that, the piece still wound up being purchased for a private collection. The low buffet (Fig. 11) is another good example of counter-productive fakery that reduces rather than improves the value of the object.

Most fakery, and particularly incompetent fakery, usually does not get very far without being spotted and identified. Unsuccessful fakery, however, is not the real problem, for sooner or later someone picks up on it. Successful fakery is that which is at least good enough to circulate and accumulate in the antiques market, undiscovered for a time, or is first identified far too late, only after one or more people have been expensively burned.

With so much fakery of Canadian antiques being inept or incompetent, or at best rather sloppy, the immediate question is how so many of these pieces got into the antiques market in the first place. How did the more incompetent of these pieces ever pass muster with even the first picker or dealer who saw them?

P. T. Barnum was again quite right when he originated that immortal phrase "There's a sucker born every minute" (1852), a guiding principle that made him a wealthy man. To that we can also add the W. C. Fields corollary "Never give a sucker an even break" (1937).

In the largely unsophisticated Canadian antiques market, even inept fakery (Figs. 10 or 11) or reproduction fakery (Figs. 26–28) succeeds, for a time, largely because too many people buy something impetuously rather than because they know it to be real or good. They get carried away with instant enthusiasm or greed in facing an apparent great bargain and forget that the first principle of caution is always to question. They ignore the basic concept of *caveat emptor*, otherwise meaning that, if you go overboard or get suckered, it's your own fault – which it is.

Another cause of ultimate distress is plain ignorance, simply not knowing, and just not being able to spot the wrong, the altered, or the fake. Many fakes or faked-up pieces get into the market and continue to circulate through many buyings and sellings – including at major auctions – just because of widespread ignorance. In an unsophisticated market, fakery can be inept or incorrect and still pass with many buyers who are simply unobservant and unaware. In a market where many decor- and fashion-oriented buyers are concerned more with appearance than substance, truly expert fakery is really unnecessary.

For some reason, people will casually acquire even a fairly expensive antique in a way they would never think of buying, say, a house or a used car, with at best a very cursory examination. I have seen people at antiques shows and in shops buy pieces of furniture without ever looking at either the backs or the undersides. I have also seen people suddenly jump into mid-bidding at auctions, apparently carried away by the heat of the moment, to bid up and buy pieces they had never even looked at during the preview. Sometimes, by sheer blind luck, this impetuous buying behaviour turns out all right. On other occasions, the buyer either pays far too much or gets stuck with a questionable piece – or both.

Fig. 10: Underneath the butchery this is a plain, but quite genuine, early-nineteenth-century pine armoire. Its value has effectively been destroyed rather than enhanced by extremely crude carving of the door panels in an effort at upgrading. The armoire, of the 1800-to-1830 era, *was* a good but simple raised-panel piece until incompetent fakers got hold of it.

As with most eighteenth- and nineteenth-century painted pieces, the armoire's original finish, a dark-red stain-paint, was totally stripped in the interests of contemporary decorating fashion. Next, an inept carver went at the door panels, shaving away surface wood to create poorly shaped relief ovals and concave-cornered crosses in the centre panels (Fig. 10a).

Finally, a truly incompetent carver had a go. By roughly chiselling down into the panels to create shallow relief surfaces, that carver then created the crude and distorted oval and round floral medallions. The surfaces of the medallions are not in actual relief, but are flush with the original panel surfaces. The wooden pins of the door frames are modern round dowels, a certain sign that the frames were taken apart and then reassembled.

Fakery as totally inept as the carving of this previously perfectly good armoire is simply destructive and, as fakery, should not pass even the most superficial inspection. As with many such pieces, however, it did, and wound up in a private collection. This is hardly the only good and genuine early Quebec armoire that has been destroyed by the hands of incompetent fakers. *Royal Ontario Museum*

Fig. 10a: A close view of a panel medallion from the armoire in Figure 10 shows the crudeness of the carving. The poorly shaped oval is not symmetrical in the panel, nor are the leaves even in size or spacing. Gouge marks are evident at the periphery of the oval, indicating how the oval medallion was created by chiselling into the surface of what was originally a plain, flat panel.

Cabinetmakers in early Quebec, and everywhere, after completing a piece to be carved, usually sent it to a professional carver or wood sculptor for completion. Wood carving was a very specialized craft, and the finest carvers made a good living doing everything from church figures and the entire interiors of churches to pieces of furniture.

The carving of the faked medallions on this armoire is far beneath eighteenth-century standards. No professional carver working on this armoire would have produced such crude work or ever delivered it to a patron. *Royal Ontario Museum*

Fig. 11: As another example of counter-productive upgrading fakery, this was once a good early-eighteenth-century Louis XIII pine low buffet, with quite genuine diamond-point door panels and plain end panels. This piece originally had straight legs, and a plain lower skirt matching the side skirts. The buffet has been brutally stripped of its original paint, down to fresh, raw wood. In its upgrading, someone first scored grooved arches into the end panels and then cut away the original skirt and inner sides of the legs into cutsey decorator-oriented "Colonial" scalloping. As an antique, the piece has effectively been ruined, and, in figuring a value, the upgrading fakery would have to be considered as unrestorable damage rather than improvement. *Royal Ontario Museum*

There are a few cardinal rules of basic caution in antiques buying that, if more people paid attention to them, would help them avoid a lot of disastrous mistakes. They have all been outlined many times before, but can always stand repeating.

1. With any piece where details, decorations, marks, or inscriptions alone either justify or substantially enhance the value – such as carving on furniture, silvermaker's marks, or presentation inscriptions – *always examine those details or decorations first.* They will likely be quite genuine, but you never know without questioning and examining. Listen to whispering inner voices and gut feelings. If the details or decorations look wrong or doubtful, then the whole piece might as well be considered wrong or doubtful.

2. No adjective-laden description, verbal provenance, attribution, or good story is any better than the antique itself. No Loyalist family history can make an 1870s Eastlake table a Loyalist-period piece. So, ignore everything else. Examine any antique and make judgements *solely on its own merits.* Watch out, as well, for passed-on "expert" opinions, which are easy to invent, misinterpret, or twist around. *The only "expert" opinion worth anything is the opinion you get directly from the "expert."*

3. *Avoid, at all costs, impulsiveness or excessive enthusiasm in buying,* which just generates carelessness and mistakes. Impetuous buying or ignorance is probably responsible for more mistakes and fakes being discovered too late than any other factor. In auctions, particularly, *never bid on anything not examined first, and thoroughly, in the sale preview.* In bidding, go into the action with the top dollar you are prepared to pay pretty firmly in mind. Remember the buyer's commission and sales taxes, for a successful bid will cost roughly 25 per cent more. Getting carried away by bidding fever is like buying groceries as an impulse shopper rather than from a list. Drop out at your predetermined highest bid and let someone else pay too much.

4. No matter how much you would like to have a particular piece, pass on it if there are unresolved questions. Likewise, as with impending surgery or buying an older house or a used car, don't hesitate to confess doubt or seek other opinions. Self-deluding pride or overconfidence is

as poor a basis for buying as ignorance or impulsiveness. *If you are not dead sure of what you are doing, simply don't do it.* It is always better to avoid a disaster than to get stuck with one.

Once the work on a fake has been completed, be it upgraded carving on a Quebec armoire or an anonymous piece of European silver with an added early Canadian marking, somehow it has to be marketed. The faker, given his clear intent to deceive and defraud, is hardly in any position to sell it directly to a collector or major dealer himself or openly to take a booth at an antiques show. The risk of discovery is too high, and there are several other safer methods that also improve the sense of provenance and authenticity.

The favoured method of passing fakes seems to be by what is termed a "plant," with several variations. The faker or, better yet, a friend or family member will make an arrangement with someone else to carry off the initial sale. This distances the fake from the faker and provides the critical first change of hands that gets the piece sold and into antiques-market circulation. The faker will usually, and most wisely, stay quite removed from the actual selling. The faker may set his own bottom-line price, what he expects to receive, and then let the seller ask for as much as he thinks he can get and keep the difference from the sale. Or the plant-seller may instead get a set percentage of the sale proceeds, with 20 to 30 per cent being typical.

Let's say the faker has just completed an upgraded Quebec armoire with bogus carved or diamond-point panels, with his too-fresh-looking work perhaps concealed by reproduced "original" paint. His friend then makes a deal with a local farmer or an old retired couple who need some extra money to do nothing more than stash the armoire in the back of their barn. The couple may very well not even know that the armoire is a fake, or who the faker is. If they suspect, they will also know the game and ask no questions. It is safer to have no incriminating knowledge.

Sitting on the barn floor, the armoire has some initial dust shaken over it, with more to accumulate. Perhaps a little straw goes on top.

Soon, quite naturally, pigeon or barn-owl droppings will come, or maybe deer mice will nest inside. That armoire is shortly going to look as if it had been stored in that barn forever. The elderly couple, for their 20- or 30-per-cent cut, are told only to call the faker's agent if a prospective buyer happens to come along. Then they all wait or, just as likely, one of them will call a known picker and plant the seed, for a finder's kickback perhaps: There might just be a really nice but so far undiscovered old armoire sitting in a barn.

Most of the older rural areas of Eastern Canada, like the eastern United States, have been and are heavily "picked" by door-to-door antique pickers who ask something such as, "Got any old junk to sell?" The regular coming of pickers, whether invited or just passing by, is still a near certainty in some long-settled areas. "Why, just mebby, m'boy. Got this old cupboard out'n th' barn. Want t' take a look?" The armoire, grotty, grungy, and maybe even smelly by this time, now looks as if it had been there since the barn was built.

The picker wants the armoire. Maybe a little added fiction from the elderly woman helps, something along the line of how they put the armoire away twenty-five, no, thirty years ago now, when her father died and they didn't need it to store the old gaffer's booze and *Playboy* magazines any more. That adds a nice touch of a provenance of long ownership.

The faker's agent on the phone, maybe billed as the old couple's son, provides a price for them to ask. The picker is appalled, since he had hoped to pick up a real gem for next to nothing. He also knows, though, that, once the piece is tarted up, he can easily get maybe twice as much. Sale completed. Cash. No paper trail; no sales taxes. Another upgraded and faked armoire goes into the antiques market.

The same plant technique can be and is used with almost any piece of furniture, and also with just about any other object.

Another Quebec favourite fake for planting is newly made rooster or chanticleer weathervane figures, of sheet iron or copper. Nicely pre-corroded, maybe even with mild rust pitting, the chanticleer gets mounted right on the plant's barn roof, as almost a come-get-me signal to pickers. Maybe a few .22-calibre bullet holes add authenticity. "Why,

I guess it's just always been there. My father remembered it even from when he was a little kid. Eighty-four, he was, when he died twenty years ago now," the plant tells the inevitable picker. Good century-long, continuous-ownership provenance. It's an ideal story, and who can question it with father dead.

The plant for fakes can also be a particularly unknowledgeable country antiques dealer, or more likely one good at acting that role, with the object being planted on a consignment basis, the dealer keeping a percentage of the sale price. Perhaps our earlier collector of the Krieghoff–Parizeau painting bought a planted piece, and artist-brother François was the actual Krieghoff faker.

Though the certainty of getting a bottom-line price is riskier, consigning the piece with a local auctioneer, though never a city or fine-art auctioneer, is another common way to plant a fake. Many rural auctioneers also double as pickers and buy pieces themselves if the price is right. These often later get included in "estate" sales, so no one is aware they were the auctioneer's own pieces. Many a faked piece has gone into the antiques market through the rural estate-auction route.

There are only three real rules of the planting technique. First, the faker should avoid also being the seller, for then he doesn't actually commit a fraud. There is nothing illegal in making or altering something, and, if someone else happens to sell it later, that's their problem. Next, the chosen plant, whether an elderly couple, a country dealer, or a picker-auctioneer, ideally should not even be aware that the piece is a fake and certainly should not know the faker. Then, deniability is actually truthful, the faker can't be traced, intent to defraud is missing, and no one can prove anything. Finally, the faked piece should never initially be exposed to any sophisticated or knowledgeable market or put at any unnecessary risk of discovery as a fake before its first sale.

The initial buyer, the picker, may be aware a piece is a fake, or at least suspect it. Pickers are hardly stupid or naïve. Still, if the fakery is good enough for the picker to buy it, he also knows he can resell it at a good profit into at least the lower levels of the antiques market. In all initial sales, of course, the transactions are in cash, with no trails of receipts, cheques, or VISA slips.

A fake or faked piece, unless it is good enough to defy detection, invariably enters the antiques market at the beginning, or first-discovery, level, and at a much lower price than it might eventually achieve. Thus, the faker is really a wholesaler to wholesalers. The fake may then circulate and trade around in the lower end of the market for months or even years, passing through numerous country antiques shops and small local antiques shows.

As mentioned earlier, many dealers quite often lack knowledge about their own inventories. They know the commercial end of what to buy and what they can sell, for that's their business. They probably also have at least a weak or superficial knowledge of styles and materials – enough for a sales pitch. With the exception of the more expert and scholarly upper-level specialized and private dealers, however, most dealers are not exactly strong on product knowledge, and not in a firm position themselves to closely examine what they are buying and selling.

Thus, unless they are good at inventing stories, the verbal provenances and attributions many dealers pass along are often just what they themselves have been told. The same is true of auction houses, which depend too much on seller-consignor information for catalogue descriptions. When it comes to fakery or upgradings, of course, ignorance is bliss. "I'm no expert. What, you think it's maybe been messed with? Why, it's just the way I got it! I never had any idea of that!" is a reasonable defence against any accusations of skulduggery.

If a fake is a halfway competent job of faking, it may well be accepted as genuine – or at least not attract negative attention – by a relatively unknowledgeable audience. Sooner or later, however, as it moves up in the market, it is also going to be noticed by some more studious and experienced dealer or collector. That moment marks the danger zone for a fake or upgraded piece, when the risk of discovery and identification becomes much greater.

Word of mouth is a primary communication device in the Canadian (or any) antiques market. At least in the upper or specialized levels of collecting, most dealers and collectors know each other. They may like or hate each other, but they have still likely had dealings with each other. Eventually, with the vast majority of upgraded or "improved"

Canadian pieces, someone is going to identify certain or probable fakery. At this point, everyone from the faker through to the first retail seller are perhaps years out of it, all with their profits, and onto other deals. In what resembles a game of musical chairs, the last owner holding the fake when the music stops is stuck with it, though perhaps only temporarily.

If the owner and the latest prospective buyer who recognized the object as fake or faked are personally friendly, or complete strangers, then the identification of the fake may very well go no further. Usually no one wants to create a fuss. The owner then gets the chance to invoke the concept of "one last buyer" and, quietly, tries to unload his mistake on someone else. Since P. T. Barnum was quite right, this may well succeed, for there always seems to be another sucker.

There is, however, also a lot of rancour from competition or sour deals, backbiting, and bad-mouthing in the antiques business, by both dealers and collectors. Thus, a fake is occasionally likely to be exposed. Particularly in the small Canadian upper-level dealer-collector community, once the phones start ringing, word of a fake can be widely spread – and quite quickly. Then the music stops and the last owner is stuck for a time. No upper-level dealer, auction house, or collector will touch the piece from then on. Dealers may disparage their competitors as skinflints, scofflaws, sleazes, or outright crooks. Still, none can afford to have their own reputations directly connected with an exposed and known fake.

The fake's unfortunate owner then has two options: keeping the piece or cutting his losses by quietly selling it back into the lower-level antiques market. That means perhaps taking a considerable loss by offering the piece through a country auctioneer or small village antiques dealer – without, of course, mentioning its certain character flaws.

Thus, the exposed fake now returns to anonymity, perhaps at a much lower price level, maybe even close to what the faker or plant originally got for it. The piece no doubt will then go the same around-and-around route it did before, until it eventually winds up with some decor-oriented end-buyer, perhaps one furnishing a recreation room with "genuine antiques."

Most fakes and faked pieces, however, even though they may be identified by numerous would-be buyers who pass without comment, never actually get exposed. Publicly exposing a fake means making an allegation based on opinion, which puts the onus on the whistle-blower to support the allegation. If the owner-seller of the fake chooses to challenge or refuses to accept the accusation that he is selling a fake, the result can be anything from an argument to endless acrimony to perhaps even litigation. No one needs that sort of hassle. Most people who spot a fake just pass on buying and, though they may comment to others enough to get the fake into the rumour mill, generally keep quiet.

Fakes, once created, never uncreate or self-destruct, nor do owners destroy them. They just go to ground for a time, perhaps in someone's home, cottage, or collection, or a dealer's storage. Ultimately, however, they will emerge again for another round, or even a fresh generation, of potential buyers.

There is nothing either mystical or magical about spotting and identifying fakes or upgradings. As in many other fields, it comes down to knowledge, experience, and, particularly, paying very close attention to minute and picky details. Identifying fakes or fakery is similar to a pathologist identifying how a deceased got that way, or a TV technician discovering why your television picture is snowy, or a mechanic isolating why your car engine is skipping and sputtering. Simply knowing what to look for and recognizing anomalies or questions when they appear are the basics of uncovering fakery.

Perhaps the real problem of fakes and fakery is not so much that individuals get stung, but what constantly accumulating fakes do to the antiques market and to the pastime of collecting as a whole. While genuine antiques are a non-renewable and slowly declining resource or commodity, fakes are the opposite. Fakes and, even more, partially faked or upgraded pieces are both steadily increasing in number and are cumulative, since more are produced year after year. Fakes, faked alterations, or reproductions in the process of becoming fakes are in constant production and, in some object categories, are flooding the market enough to make buyers suspicious of even genuine pieces.

Over a number of decades, the sheer quantity of fakes accumulating in the market can come to outweigh the remaining numbers of the real and genuine. In a few categories, such as Indian trade silver, blacksmith-made iron, scrimshaw, and some forms of pine furniture, this has already happened. Then the potential buyer is put in a position of *presuming* a piece is likely fake or faked – because the odds now are that it is – at least until he or she can somehow establish otherwise.

Compounding the problem is the fact that even mediocre fakes improve with age, and eventually become age-defined, or Definition-1, antiques in their own right. The longer a fake or faked piece circulates, and the older it gets, as the work sees usage and mellows with time, the more difficult it becomes to determine and be certain that it is a fake. The problem, again, is the same as that facing a pathologist trying to determine the cause of death of a decomposed body or a skeleton, as opposed to a fresh corpse. Evidence softens and declines with age. With certain types of fakes or upgrading fakery, as with some reproductions, once fifty years or another century has passed, in many cases it will likely become impossible to make really solid determinations at all.

With many categories of English and European antiques, a necessary presumption of fakery was reached decades ago. The situation is not as bad in Canada, quite yet, simply because the fakery business is newer and is still limited to a relatively small market. Not as much past fakery has had the chance to accumulate in the Canadian market as in Europe or Britain. Even here, however, in the few categories outlined above, fakes or faked pieces may already comprise a sizeable percentage of what is on the market at any time. As genuine antiques decline in quantity, and fakes, fakery, and reproductions continue to proliferate and accumulate in the market, the situation can only get worse.

3

Hoaxes and Humbugs:
Tales from the Trenches

—◆·▸◆◀·◆—

"The world is made up for the most part of fools and knaves."
— George Villiers, Duke of Buckingham, 1671

Having outlined the how and why of fakery in the previous chapter, this is now best illustrated with some tales from the combat zone. The range of fakery, and the scope of possibilities for faking, is really infinite. No one has seen it all. There are always new twists, and even after some forty years in the field, I never get through a year without running across things I've never encountered before.

Most people, even collectors, when they hear the word "fake," immediately think of art, not three-dimensional antiques. However, very little Canadian art, with the exception of the works of a handful of artists, has been faked. In part this is because the price levels for most artists in the Canadian market simply do not justify the time and effort that must go into trying to copy the style and techniques of other artists. A good fake, after all, involves not just copying another artist's existing pictures, but also creating new and previously unknown works "in the style and manner of."

Some Canadian artists have also kept and left inventories and records of their own work, while art historians have substantially recorded the work of others. Thus, a newly discovered and previously unknown picture by a well-known artist whose works are recorded would be suspicious to any but the most naïve if it suddenly came on the market. The upper-price-range Canadian art market is too small for that. Thus, most Canadian artists are unfakeable on a practical level, for the reasons mentioned.

Art fakers with any real talent and skill, who are able successfully to copy or emulate the work of other artists, are but a few in number at any time. Artists capable of faking successfully are certainly also capable of producing and successfully marketing their own work. The trouble is that those artists may be unknown or minor names in their own right, making marketing of their own work difficult and their prices low. Fakery of established or famous names, as with any other antique, can be far more lucrative. To fakers as to bank robbers, a life of crime may not be due to the favourite rationales of parental, educational, economic, or societal deprivation but, as some criminal analysts would admit, a deliberate career choice.

Only one Canadian artist, Dutch-born Cornelius Krieghoff (1815–1872), has ever achieved the international acceptance and contemporary price levels necessary to be worth massive faking. Fakes are known of other Canadian artists, but not nearly to the extent of Krieghoff fakes.

Really good art or antiques fakers are like anyone else with ambition; if you've got the talent, exploit it. This further explains why so few Canadian artists are faked. Why should a good art faker, capable of successfully following the styles and techniques of other artists, bother with faking artists bringing $5,000 or $10,000 in the current art market when he can put his talents into faking $50,000 or $100,000 artists?

Two of the greatest art fakers of recent years known to have faked Canadian artists were Tom Keating (1917–1984) and Elmyr de Hory (1911–1976). Both were competent artists who painted in their own right. De Hory, for his fakes, specialized primarily though not wholly in modern masters such as Picasso, Matisse, and Modigliani. Keating, however, had a much broader scope, faking a number of artists, and was able to do oils, watercolours, and drawings. When Keating was finally exposed in 1976, he subsequently went public and confessed all, and even wrote his autobiography, *The Fake's Progress* (1977).

Fig. 12: Cornelius Krieghoff (1815–1872) has the dubious honour of being the most faked of any early Canadian artist. Various authorities have estimated the number of existing Krieghoff fakes at from three to four times the number of genuine Krieghoff paintings.

This cabin in the Laurentians, with a woman in the doorway, is somewhat in a Krieghoff style, but by a painter who was much better at background landscape than at foreground detail or figures. The painting, probably by some nineteenth-century art student, or perhaps even two people, is clearly not Krieghoff's work. The signature, "C. Krieghoff/1868" in the lower left corner, was certainly added much more recently. *Royal Ontario Museum*

Elmyr de Hory, self-exiled to the Spanish island of Ibitza, faked mostly in the direction of modern Impressionists. As a friend of writer Clifford Irving, de Hory was uncovered during the great scandal over Irving's fake "autobiography" of the reclusive Howard Hughes. He was exposed by Irving in his own autobiography, *Fake*, in 1969. De Hory admitted to having faked both Group of Seven artists, such as A.Y. Jackson, and Krieghoff, but the numbers he did remain unknown. No one knows where most of Keating's or de Hory's work is today, but, including the Krieghoffs and Jacksons, it is all still out there in the art market somewhere.

Among the approximately three thousand fakes Keating claimed to have produced, he admitted to some two hundred Krieghoffs, at least some of which have no doubt found their way to Canada. When the late J. Russell Harper was cataloguing all of Krieghoff's known work, of some twelve hundred pictures he examined, he found that at least eight hundred were fakes, or at least "wrong." Max Stern of the Dominion Gallery in Montreal believed that, by the mid-1970s, there were probably four fake Krieghoffs to every one of the artist's genuine paintings. Some, of course, were done by contemporary students or copyists and were only quasi-competent works in spite of their Krieghoff signatures. Most are readily identifiable as copies or fakes (Fig. 12).

During the sixteenth to nineteenth centuries, before the establishment of formal art schools, artists took on students exactly as cabinetmakers and silversmiths took on apprentices, to help in their studios and bring in extra money. Artist-teachers, including Krieghoff, often taught by having students copy their own work, and today's art market, in Canada and everywhere, is full of nineteenth-century student copies, particularly landscapes. Sometimes artists touched up the work of their better students, and on occasion even signed their own names. Copying is still a teaching technique; witness the art students with portable easels often seen in art museums.

Actual cases of prosecution for art forgery and fraud are rare in Canada, for the fakes are usually impossible to trace to their sources and the cases are thus very difficult to establish and prove in court.

Usually the best the law can do, once a fake is identified and exposed, is to charge the last dealer who sold it. Even then, intent to defraud has to be proved. Did the dealer accused or charged actually *know* the fake was a fake, and deliberately misrepresent it as genuine, or was the dealer himself unaware?

The famous Routhier case of 1977 in Montreal involved tracing a number of fake A. Y. Jackson and Robert Pilot paintings back through a series of transactions. In the end, just one dealer, Réjean-Guy Routhier, was convicted of fraudulently selling the paintings, but the actual faker has never been identified. That is far more usual than fakers who confess. Good fakers usually don't talk.

In introducing the various forms of fakery, it is also necessary to mention pure hoaxes, fakes made as jokes or put-ons, without any primary financial motivation. Thus, I thought I might relate the story of a recent and great American hoax, accomplished by a fake. It was an absolute classic, which fooled everyone for quite a long time.

No doubt the vast majority of faking is done for financial gain, but that is not always the case. Fakes are occasionally produced for other reasons, sometimes as pure hoaxes, just for the challenge. Some fakers have enjoyed simply seeing one of their creations launched and then sitting back to revel in the fun as chaos erupts on the fake's discovery and exposure.

Certainly the most recent grand antiques hoax was the making of the "Great Brewster Chair." This was an English-derived form of a heavy spindled chair, of which only two famous American-made early Massachusetts examples are now known to exist. One was made in the 1620s by John Alden for William Brewster, and another in the 1650s by an unknown maker. For decades, rumours had circulated in the American antiques market of a third surviving Brewster chair, though it had yet to be discovered.

In the late 1960s, a Rhode Island master cabinetmaker and wood sculptor, Armand LaMontagne, decided to test and, he hoped, confound "the experts," who in past encounters he had found rather arrogant. Over a two-month period he built a third Brewster chair, very carefully using seventeenth-century methods. Then, in a lengthy and laborious "antiquing" process of bleaching, staining, burning, dusting, smoking, and inflicting deliberate damage, LaMontagne created the perfect three-century-old reproduction. It took more work – and longer – to "antique" the chair than to make it.

He then gave the chair to a friend in Maine who was an occasional picker and dealer to dealers. Dealers came and examined, and in 1970 the Maine friend finally sold the chair for $500. It then changed hands several times, moving upward in the antiques market as such pieces do, at ever higher prices. In 1971, it was finally acquired by dealer Roger Bacon of New Hampshire, who specialized in American colonial-period furniture. Bacon, satisfied that the chair was genuine, offered and sold it for about $9,500 to the Henry Ford Museum in Dearborn, Michigan.

While the Henry Ford Museum had the chair on display, crowing more than a little over the greatest antiques discovery and coup of the century, rumours began to circulate that maybe the chair wasn't quite right, that maybe it was even a fake. LaMontagne himself was the source of the rumours, bragging around about the chair he had made.

The Henry Ford Museum dismissed the rumours. Roger Bacon, from whom they had bought the chair, had been satisfied, though when doubts arose he offered to buy it back. The museum had itself checked and rechecked the chair, and also remained satisfied. In case his claim itself was suspected as a hoax, however, LaMontagne had kept sawed-off sections of the spindles and leg bottoms. The wood-grain ends, if ever compared, would match like fingerprints. He had also left some deliberate hidden clues in the bottoms of drilled holes, but no one had ever gone so far as to totally disassemble the chair.

The Henry Ford Museum finally removed the chair from display in 1977 "for further examination," just as the story, with photographs of LaMontagne's "Great Brewster Chair," broke in a newspaper article (Fig. 13). The chair went into storage and has never reappeared since.

In spite of rumblings and threats, LaMontagne had committed no crime in making the chair and giving it to a friend and had not

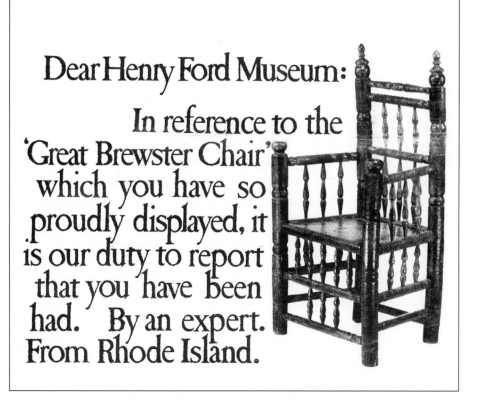

Dear Henry Ford Museum:

In reference to the 'Great Brewster Chair' which you have so proudly displayed, it is our duty to report that you have been had. By an expert. From Rhode Island.

Fig. 13: In a classic hoax, in the late 1960s cabinetmaker Armand LaMontagne of Rhode Island made a wholly new seventeenth-century "Great Brewster Chair," which he elaborately "antiqued" by a number of complex methods (Chapter 3). Though a total fake, the chair passed even the closest examination and wound up being purchased by the Henry Ford Museum, which exhibited the piece with great fanfare. Through purchase, gift, or bequest, virtually all older and larger museums have inadvertently (or deliberately, for teaching purposes) acquired a few fakes over the decades. LaMontagne exposed his own fake in this 1977 issue of the *Rhode Islander* newspaper magazine, with its headline in seventeenth-century type. *Author files*

benefited from any of its sales. Having blown the whistle on his own fake, he was happy with having had the last and loudest laugh. He subsequently made another "Great Brewster Chair" – for himself.

As mentioned earlier, on only a few occasions have I ever seen freshly made and new pieces of *totally* fake Canadian furniture, pieces actually made for marketing as genuine, though there are many made-up pieces and older close reproductions on the market that get sold as genuine (Figs. 26–28). Occasionally I am called on by auction houses such as Sotheby's to render my humble opinion on pieces that have come in for potential consignment. Auction houses do not knowingly sell fakes, though it sometimes happens unknowingly. Selling fakes is bad for their credibility and reputations.

On one memorable occasion, the piece had already been delivered and was actually in Sotheby's storeroom, so I had more than just the usual pre-consignment photograph to look at. Sotheby's was uncertain, for good reason. The piece was a very nice chest of drawers of mixed bird's-eye and curly maple, combined with cherry. The hopeful consignor had stated that the chest had come from the Brockville, Ontario, area and dated from around 1840. No provenance or history of ownership was offered with it. The chest was totally proper and very well made, largely with hand tools, with quite correct secondary pine for the drawers and good, tight hand-cut dovetailing.

The trouble was that the piece, though in a 1830s-to-1840s style, was absolutely new. Unlike LaMontagne's "Great Brewster Chair," there had been no attempt at artificial wear or aging. Even the inevitably worn drawer-side-bottom-to-drawer-runner contact was square and fresh. The chest had not had its drawers pulled in and out a dozen times since it was made.

The sealer-finish appeared to be just a clear shellac over the light yellow-white of recently planed and sanded maple, with no signs of any age patina or darkening from many decades of air and light exposure. The faker in this case had done a beautiful job of design and construction, and in a sophisticated and well-equipped shop. Then, unlike most fakers, he had just stopped there for some strange reason, with no further attempt at "antiquing" or trying to make the piece really appear as if it dated from the 1840s.

I reported to Sotheby's that the chest seemed virtually new, hardly 1840s, or even 1940s. The consignor defended the piece as genuine, now offering the idea that it had been a seldom-used guest-room piece, and had been recently refinished. Since there were still no signs of age or use, and no provenance beyond the present ownership, that story held no water. The piece was obviously new, so perhaps the consignor was a plant and agent for the faker. There was no way to know. I finally had to do a written report, with a copy to the consignor. Sotheby's refused the consignment and declined to sell the chest.

The probable faker or plant in this case made the mistake of trying to launch the maple chest into the market at too high a level, a level at which it ran a great risk of being too closely examined, whether by Sotheby's, me, or someone else. The piece was simply not up to that sort of attention. As with most such fakes, the chest quickly submerged, no doubt later to resurface elsewhere.

Perhaps the most audacious single fake I have ever experienced I still call "The Mystery of the Schindler Plate." It was audacious not just in what it was and the way it evolved, but in the fact that its owner, agent, or plant was trying to sell it directly into the museum or upper-end collector level of the antiques market. The plate's story is well worth relating.

Alain Hébert (not his real name) was a picker. He was a short and rotund French Canadian in his fifties, who spoke quite adequate English, and had driven to Toronto from central Quebec. With him was his wife, of identical shape, a bottle blonde in lime-green slacks, who was so quiet that I was aware she spoke only French.

Hébert had with him a silver plate, about ten inches (25 cm) in diameter. It was quite a handsome piece, though not engraved or otherwise decorated. On its bottom was the JS punch-mark of Joseph Schindler, a Montreal silversmith from 1760 to 1786, and of his widow, who had continued his business after his death. Schindler silver is rare, and his widow's pieces even more so.

"This one's a Widow Schindler piece," Hébert insisted. "Probably 1790s. I got it about three months ago. One of the best pieces I've ever found." He was, of course, trying to justify the $3,500 he was asking for it. For a good and rare piece of eighteenth-century Canadian silver, $3,500 is nothing today, but twenty-five years ago $3,500 was a very stiff price for an undecorated Quebec silver plate, in spite of its rare mark.

Pickers come up with rare or fine pieces only by great luck, for they are more pack-rat buyers. Family castoffs, old furniture, and household pieces with the cachet of some age but few if any other virtues are their bread-and-butter business. The Schindler plate, on the other hand, looked like a church piece and had perhaps once been part of a communion service. So, where had Hébert acquired it? Pickers are notoriously closed-mouthed, except for their sales pitches, so I knew it was pointless to ask the question. Possibly directly from a church?

Quebec village priests in poor rural parishes had been selling off their church silver for decades. Though they really had no right to sell it, if the church roof leaked, it had to be fixed. Fixing roofs costs money. Ever since the 1930s, a lot of church silver by eighteenth-century Quebec makers had passed into the antiques market, via pickers, directly from churches.

As I turned the Schindler plate back and forth in my hands, something about it just didn't quite come together. I wanted a better chance to examine it, and without Hébert sitting there giving me his non-stop sales patter and grinning, waiting for me to say, "Yes, we'll take it."

I told Hébert I wanted to look at the plate more closely. "Why don't you and your wife go for lunch, and maybe go shopping in Yorkville, and come back about two. By then I should know whether the plate is for us." He agreed to that, and I gave him a receipt.

The minute they walked down the stairs, I called John Langdon. John was then certainly the foremost collector of Canadian silver (who later gave the Royal Ontario Museum his entire collection) and the author of the two best books on Canadian silver. I am no silver specialist, and I often called John about problem pieces. I told him about the Schindler plate that had just walked in. He perked right up and said he was on his way.

The plate, as I picked it up again, was unusually heavy for a Canadian piece. Because early Canadian silversmiths depended for their metal on old and battered scrap silver and illegally melted-down coins, Canadian silver is usually very thin and light. Neither did I like the plate's rim. The rim looked as if it had perhaps been shaved, made narrower from a wider rim, and then carefully polished and buffed.

The JS punch-mark in the base was perfect – too perfect. The plate itself had seen much polishing over two centuries. The mark had been polished over, too, so the edges of the letters were somewhat dulled, but not to the extent of the plate. Under my ten-power magnifying glass, the mark still looked somewhat too crisp.

Quite a lot of what seemed to be European silver was appearing in Quebec in the late 1960s and 1970s, either originally unmarked or with European marks ground away and polished off, leaving slight depressions. This anonymous silver then acquired Canadian punch-marks, usually of rare Quebec makers. I already had a strong suspicion that Hébert's plate was a recently imported French piece, perhaps early nineteenth century but originally unmarked, that had acquired its Schindler mark within the past few months. Whether Hébert himself was behind it, I didn't know at the time.

Some newly added marks on silver either vary slightly from the known original marks (Figs. 46, 46a) or the style and date of the silver does not match the original dates of the mark used. Sometimes, too, the faking job is not quite completed to perfection. On other pieces, though, like this would-be Schindler plate, the changes are very, very good and the faking is hard to pin down absolutely. That was why I wanted John Langdon to look at it.

John agreed with my suspicions. "The plate looks original enough by itself. Late eighteenth century, or more likely early nineteenth. Probably French, maybe German. I think the rim's perhaps been shaved just a little, likely to smooth out some old dents and gouges. I agree that the mark's suspicious at best, and the mark has to be fake if the plate itself is European. I've heard rumbles that a dental technician near

Loretteville is making reproduction punch-stamps and, if this is one of his, he's pretty good."

"So, you think the punch is as good as the original?" I asked.

"Better. Just too good," John responded. "I've seen quite a few Schindler-marked pieces, though never a plate. If it wasn't for the plate being the wrong style for the mark, mid-Empire instead of Louis XV, the mark by itself might fool me. It's good, but, as you say, just too fresh-looking."

Then John pointed out something else. Joseph Schindler had used a simple JS punch-mark, like the one on this plate. His widow, in continuing the business after 1786 and until 1802, had used her husband's punch *plus* a small MONTREAL mark, less than an inch (2.5 cm) long. Every Widow Schindler piece John had ever seen had had the JS and that little MONTREAL punch-mark. The style of the plate dated more from 1800 to maybe 1820, well after Joseph Schindler's death, which was probably one reason why Hébert was trying to sell it as a later and rarer Widow Schindler piece.

"Notice!" said John, dramatically flipping the plate over. "No MONTREAL mark!"

Hébert had told me he was going on to Detroit if we didn't take the plate, to try the Detroit Institute of Arts, which had a very good French-Canadian collection. Hébert had some other Quebec silver with him, but none of it was of much interest to us with our already large collection.

John wanted to be gone before the Héberts came back. We left it that I'd tell Hébert I didn't think this was a Widow Schindler piece, or worth the asking price, because of the lack of the MONTREAL stamp. I would not tell him, however, that John had also looked at the plate or that we were convinced it was a fake.

Meanwhile, I would put out the word and alert the few museums, including the National Gallery and Detroit, that might acquire such a piece. John would take care of the serious and high-value collector contingent, which numbered then no more than about a dozen people. Essentially, we would quietly try to make the plate unsaleable. Then we would sit back and wait, for John was convinced we would hear of this plate again.

The Héberts returned from lunch. I told them just what John and

I had cooked up. I didn't think the plate, *without* a MONTREAL mark, was by the Widow Schindler, and the plate was not for us. They left, taking away the plate, and I never again heard from Alain Hébert.

As sure as a bounced cheque, five months later the plate came back. It was not with Hébert this time, but with Henry Pellam (not his real name), a young novice but fast-learning Canadian silver collector whom I'd met a few times before. "This is coming up at an auction in Montreal next month," Henry reported. "I heard about it because my brother-in-law is co-owner of the auction house. He loaned it to me for a couple of days, in case I want to go for it."

He unwrapped the plate as if it were the Holy Grail and handed it to me. "Kind of strange," he said. "I showed it to John Langdon last night. All he did was crack up laughing. Didn't tell me anything, and said to bring it to you; you were the 'real expert.'" Beyond a doubt it was the same Schindler plate that I'd seen five months before.

I turned it over. Henry watched my smile turn to shock. John was putting me on. Then, just as John had, I cracked up as well. I couldn't help it. Hébert had followed what in hindsight I guess amounted to my instructions. I didn't even need my magnifying glass. The pristine JS punch-mark was still there. And there as well, below the JS, was now a new and perfect three-quarter-inch-long (2-cm-long) MONTREAL mark, also polished over and slightly worn. The Widow Schindler had struck again, to be sure.

As I re-examined the plate, with its added new mark, I told Henry Pellam the whole story, beginning with Hébert, the picker, and gave him a quick lecture on fakery. Of all the many fakes I have seen, however, the Schindler plate was memorable, for it's the only fake I've ever seen that was still evolving and growing as I watched its travels.

Henry Pellam had his brother-in-law reject the plate for his auction, so perhaps Alain Hébert still has his – or some other faker's – creation. On the other hand, P.T. Barnum was absolutely right, and Hébert may well have moved it on. No silver-collecting museum, however, or any private collector I know, has ever since heard of the Schindler plate.

Another form of faked silver emerged more recently. Ritchie's auction house in Toronto brought us a silver serving spoon and a large silver soup ladle, both of which appeared suspicious to them. They were handsome pieces, both with the LA punch-mark of Laurent Amiot (Quebec, 1764–1838). As with the Schindler plate, however, the marks were very good – just a little too good.

As I looked at the backs of the handles, I noticed that both pieces had three or four very small discoloured spots, not pitting or tarnish, but spots just a little brighter than the surrounding metal. What had caused the spots? None of us had run across anything like this before.

Usually, in altering silver and adding fake marks, any old but less-valuable marks are carefully ground and polished away. That technique, however, always leaves small and shallow depressions. Though the depressions left by erasing previous marks may not always be visible, they can usually be felt with the fingertips.

In the case of the "Amiot" ladle and spoon, we quickly decided that the faker had filled in the earlier marks instead. The pieces themselves were quite genuine, probably English or European, and with original but now-unknown marks that the faker had decided were less valuable than Amiot marks. With a tiny jeweller's torch and fine silver solder, the faker had filled in the earlier punch-marks instead of grinding them off. After a final smoothing and polishing, nothing now showed but the discoloured spots.

The faker had forgotten one little detail, however, which destroyed the success of his products. The early Canadian silversmiths had no source of newly mined silver and depended instead on melting down old silver and coinage of many origins. Though some of that silver may have been "coin" content (.975), none of it was chemically pure silver, and some of the early coins melted down were as little as .800 (or 80 per cent) silver. Thus, all early Canadian silver included trace amounts of other metals, such as copper, cadmium, arsenic, tin, or whatever, that caused very slight variations in colour. The colour variations are rarely noticeable in the absence of a close contrast.

Modern jewellers' silver solder, however, is either "sterling" silver (.925) or "coin" silver, virtually pure. The variable colour of early silver, given its unknown real content, cannot be well matched unless the silver used for repairs or alterations is of roughly the same content. The silver solder used to infill the old marks on the spoon and ladle was purer in content, perhaps "coin," than the pieces themselves, and thus left the telltale contrasting brighter spots where the original marks had been.

Ritchie's, in the end, sold the ladle and spoon, but described both as anonymous pieces with altered marks. Since neither was a specially high-value piece, even after the alterations and new marks, I wondered why the faker had bothered.

With some English faked silver, and the occasional Canadian piece, genuine punch-marks from a lesser piece like a teaspoon are carefully cut out and lifted. The marks are then inserted and soldered into a much more major and valuable object, such as a serving tureen. This marrying takes infinite skill and care, and can be virtually invisible – until a slight heating or an oblique light exposes the colour of the fine soldering. The mark-transferring technique, however, as opposed to new fake punch-marks, is so difficult to accomplish that it is only rarely used in creating fake Canadian silver. I have, in fact, seen such a piece only once, though there are undoubtedly others.

Some years ago I sat through an upscale auction that featured, among other goodies, a handsome silver bowl purporting to be by a well-known early-nineteenth-century Maritimes maker. The marks appeared quite genuine, and undoubtedly were. During the previews, it took me two separate examinations to come to a firm opinion. The bowl was perfect – almost. In spite of much smoothing and polishing, there still remained very slight traces of jeweller's-torch soldering around the maker's marks, both inside and on the base. The soldering traces showed only in slanting light, but why were they there at all? On a smooth surface, there was nothing there that might have needed repairs, and no other good reason for the soldering.

A dealer acquaintance had spotted this, too, and, in fact, had stimulated my second examination. We could only conclude that the maker's marks had been lifted and inserted. The faker had apparently cut apart a genuinely marked piece, but one of much lower value, probably a teaspoon. He had then cut into the bowl, expertly inserted and soldered in the genuine marks from the teaspoon handle, and then carefully, but not quite carefully enough, buffed and polished over his work. To accomplish a job of that skill, the faker was himself almost certainly a professional jeweller or silversmith.

Our doubts about that bowl were just considered opinions, based on hasty auction-preview examinations, though not necessarily fact. Perhaps there was some valid reason for soldering traces that we could not rationalize. Still, others in the audience must have also thought the bowl was "wrong," for they stayed away from it as well. It sold for just its probable reserve, less than half of its catalogued low estimate. It would have brought far more had suspicions been fewer and bidding more active. No one, however, actually mentioned that the bowl might be a fake, and presumably it is still somewhere in the market.

The marking of anonymous silver with Canadian makers' punch-stamps, the erasing of original marks and remarking, or the lifting and reinserting of genuine marks has been going on with Canadian silver at least since the early 1960s. Some is extremely and cleverly well done, making positive identification of the best fakes a very uncertain proposition. Usually, but not invariably, fake maker markings are confined to relatively high-value pieces, and the majority of fakery is of eighteenth-century Quebec makers' marks on church, rather than domestic, silver.

Conversely, except for the Ritchie's pieces, I have never seen or even suspected a fake Canadian maker's mark on simple flatware, such as spoons or forks, or small pieces, such as snuffboxes, sugar tongs, or salt cellars. These usually sell in the hundreds rather than thousands of dollars and are not sufficiently high-priced to be worth faking. Likewise, I have only occasionally seen or heard of fake Canadian silver markings on pieces made by other than early Quebec makers. Equally good and well-known silversmiths from the Maritimes or Upper Canada, such as Peter Nordbeck (1789–1861) of Halifax or William Stennet (—1822–1847—) of Toronto, so far seem under-represented though hardly absent in the rogues' gallery of faked Canadian silver.

Fake markings of well-known Canadian makers on high-value silver are always a risk and should always be suspected and looked for. To a really proficient silver or jewellery maker, very little is impossible.

If a piece of silver is genuine and otherwise as it should be, and its design and style period match the date range for the marking, no one can always be absolutely certain of identifying a fake marking. Often, however, there is something else wrong as well. Even to John Langdon, the giveaways with the Schindler plate were that the style and the date of the plate were too late for the claimed maker, and the mark was also incomplete for that maker. The JS mark that *was* initially there was virtually perfect. Similar inconsistencies emerge with the supposed Landron plate (Fig. 46).

If I was presented today with an early and fine Canadian maker-marked piece of church or table silver for sale – the type of silver most likely to have a faked marking – and if I had the slightest doubt, I would take refuge in provenance. I wouldn't touch it without knowing where it had been and who had owned it, *and was able to check that*, for the last forty years or so, or from before the age of fakery. With antiques such as high-value Canadian church silver, the fakers have now had forty years of experience, and their work has accumulated past work, every piece of it out there in collections or somewhere in the antiques market. With categories of antiques like expensive Quebec church silver that carry a particularly high risk of fakery, prospective buyers today should almost *presume* they are fake and then go about trying to establish otherwise.

Another silver type, Indian trade silver, is riddled with fakes and reproductions, in this case new and wholly made-up pieces (Fig. 34). Trade silver is nothing but very thin, flat silver sheet, cut in the form of crosses, small round pins and fasteners, arm bands, bracelets, head-bands, badges, and necklace gorgets. Much is crudely engraved with thin lines, and sometimes with animal symbols representing tribes or clans. Trade silver was used both in the actual fur trade, where it was traded for skins, and as political gifts, handed out to chiefs and other Indian dignitaries by both traders and agents of the British Indian Department.

Trade silver comes in two forms. The Hudson's Bay Company, operating in the north through posts on Hudson and James bays, used English-made trade silver brought in on HBC supply ships each spring. The English-HBC silver is often unmarked and is typically punch-marked by makers only on more elaborate pieces. The southern fur trade, covering the Great Lakes and west, was controlled from Montreal, particularly by the North West Company. The southern fur trade used largely Montreal- and Quebec-made trade silver, of which much was maker-marked. The prime, though hardly the only, contractor to the North West Company, with the most common marking, seems to have been Robert Cruickshank (—1767–1809—) of Montreal, with his familiar script RC punch.

Trade silver, in its usually simple forms, is quite easy to punch or cut out of sheet silver and to form and finish, and is equally easy to decorate, usually with an electric engraving or hand-held "vibro" tool. In the 1970s and early 1980s, an Ontario group flooded the market with unmarked fakes and occasional pieces with Montreal or Quebec marks. Trade-silver fakes, simple unmarked pieces, polished and artificially worn, can be difficult to detect with any certainty. The fakes also include apparently invented forms unknown in genuine Indian trade silver and have never been found in any known archaeological context.

Probably well over half of the trade silver that appears on the market today is fake or reproduction. I have seen one western private collection, formed over the past fifteen years, where no less than 50 per cent of the pieces are at least suspect. Most trade silver has floated through the antiques and "Indian artefacts" shows and markets, including auctions, changing hands many times, and has no provenance. Even with trade silver that is genuine, much has been illegally excavated by "pot-hunters," and the locations or provenances concealed. Many other pieces, genuine and fake alike, have acquired completely fictional location and excavation-site histories. Thus, Indian trade silver that is offered for sale, perhaps even more than Quebec church silver, should be presumed to be fake unless the buyer can reasonably establish otherwise.

"Married" pieces, as outlined earlier, are blends of similar components or parts from at least two different original pieces. Usually they are two-sectioned chests of drawers, desk-bookcases, or two-tiered cupboards or buffets (Figs. 14, 15), all pieces which were often originally made in two parts. Over the generations, furniture sections sometimes got separated. They could get lost or badly damaged in moving. Some house imperative such as a low ceiling could dictate the use of only a bottom section, and the upper part has been disposed of or lost. Sometimes wills even divided two-sectioned pieces between two heirs, as has often happened with sets of chairs. Only by chance and very rarely do such separated pieces ever come back together.

A married piece does not necessarily need to be two-sectioned, however. It can easily be an armoire case, with its original doors missing, that gets fitted with other quite genuine doors, perhaps salvaged from a built-in cupboard in a house being demolished. A married piece can equally well be a cherry or mahogany drop-leaf table that acquires a top and leaves from another table. It can be the separate "banquet" extensions for a dining table. There are many possible variations.

Given enough similarity between segments or sections of originally different pieces of furniture, a clever and skilled cabinetmaker can marry them into a single piece, and the alterations are sometimes very difficult to detect.

As just one example, the board of an Ontario historic-house museum, before seeking any advice, had committed to and already partially paid for an English mahogany secretary-desk of perhaps 1790 to 1820. Only then did they approach me to examine the piece; at the same time they called in a very good furniture conservator and restorer. We looked at the piece separately, and both came quite independently to the conclusion that the secretary-desk was a married piece.

The mahogany of the lower desk and upper bookcase section, in grain and colour, was virtually identical, making the pieces a good match. The sides and shelves of the upper section, however, were thinner than those of the lower desk. Though we could not disassemble and up-end the sections with the piece sitting in a dealer's shop, we

Fig. 14: A typical "married" piece, this Ontario secretary-desk is a blending of two separate sections that are not original to each other. Both sections are of cherry, and of the 1850-to-1860 period, but there the similarities end. In material and construction, there are many differences of detail between the two. Beyond that, the upper bookcase section is wider than the desk top, something never encountered with an original two-sectioned piece. The overhanging round-edged desk top itself, however, is also a modern replacement, and different from the probable original top. The backboards of the two units are of original wide boards, but are also quite different (Fig. 14a).

There is, in fact, no evidence that this desk originally had an upper bookcase unit at all, and considerable evidence that it did not. Thus, as a two-sectioned secretary-desk, the balance of probabilities is that the whole piece is likely a complete fabrication, composed of a perfectly original but separate slant-front desk, to which a completely separate bookcase unit has been fitted and married. *Royal Ontario Museum*

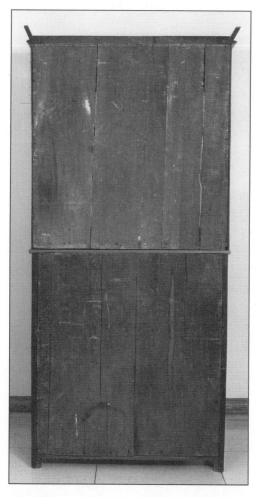

Fig. 14a: The back of the secretary-desk in Figure 14 shows the details that indicate the recent marrying of this piece. The differences in backboards, saw marks, and colours of age-patina darkening are quite evident. The lighter boards of the upper section are edge-butted, and most show the curved blade marks of a post-1860s rotary saw. The darker-coloured boards of the lower desk have hand-planed tongue-and-groove edges, all with the straight blade marks of a gang saw.

The sides of the desk and bookcase unit are of different thicknesses. The frame or case of the upper bookcase section is slightly *wider* than the desk frame. The desk top is a recent addition, showing as new wood, and is extended beyond the desk sides to accommodate the slightly wider upper unit. Finally, there is no provision for positioning or attaching the bookcase section to the desk top except for three recently drilled screw holes for the screws that hold the unit from underneath. *Royal Ontario Museum*

Fig. 15: As a miscellaneous assembly or made-up piece, this two-piece open-shelved pine cupboard, presumed to be from Quebec, combines segments or parts from several partial pieces and shows the work of more than one hand. The lower section began life as a very simple carpenter-made low buffet with two drawers, of the 1860-to-1880 period. The open-shelved upper section, of the same period but originally from a quite different piece, was married to the buffet fairly recently. The original low buffet at that point became a married two-section cupboard.

The cupboard, however, includes other work beyond just the marrying. The convex scalloping below the top-section cornice, as well as the New England-style concave cutouts of the cupboard sides between shelves, are all recent "improvements," or upgradings, and were probably done either when the sections were married or sometime later.

In the base section of the original buffet, the bracket base and feet are recent additions. The present drawers are also replacements; the originals were probably lost at some point. The door panels are replacements as well, but wrongly shaped, with the wood grain running horizontally. The grain of original door panels always ran vertically. The door framing also shows considerable wear at the upper centre, though this is not reflected in the panels. Thus, the cupboard is a totally made-up fake, with its added and upgraded top section, its new bracket base and feet, and its replaced drawers and door panels. The cupboard is, all at once, a fake, a married piece, and a made-up miscellaneous assemblage. The hardware is reproduction. *Private collection* noticed that the bookcase shelves and top had a look of having been cut down, as if the upper section had once been wider than it was now, and had then been fitted, or married, to the desk. The rough back-boards of the two sections, though original, were also quite different in widths and saw-blade marks, a common indicator that the desk and bookcase had come from two different pieces.

We reported separately, and both of us recommended that the historic house recover its deposit and not buy this secretary-desk for placement in a museum context. In a private home-furnishing situation, a well-done married piece is all right, as long as the owners know what it is. In a historic-house or museum context, we felt originality should be a prerequisite for acquisitions. Enough members of the historic-house board liked the secretary-desk, however, that, in spite of knowing it was a married piece, they bought it anyway.

As mentioned earlier, marriage has an opposite number, known as "divorce." Dealers sometimes wind up with a partial piece or a section of furniture for which they cannot find a suitable marriage partner. The tactic then is to complete a divorce. Lower sections acquire new tops (Fig. 14), to appear as if they had always been single-unit pieces. Upper sections of chests of drawers, cupboards, or bookcases also acquire new bases and feet, to become small free-standing armoires, glass-door cabinets, or single-unit, rather than two-tiered, chests of drawers.

Marrying two or three different and separate parts of only partial pieces, or completing divorces with new tops or bases – but always blended together to make intact and saleable objects, whether it is furniture or whatever – is fairly common practice, particularly among dealers. Dealers are the most likely to have accumulated large inventories, sometimes barns or warehouses full, including all manner of parts and pieces and useful junk. A dealer with a partial piece, even if he lacks another partial piece to marry with it, often knows one or more other dealers, who are also likely to have barnloads. The dealer will likely find what he needs for a marriage or, if not, there is always divorce, by applying a new top or base.

Consider the two-tiered buffet in Figure 17, which is quite genuine except for its upgraded carving. If the top of that piece was removed,

Fig. 16: Original carved decoration on early Quebec furniture, exactly as in France, always stood in relief. The design or motif was first sketched out on the surface of the wood. Surrounding wood was then carefully chiselled and shaved away, to leave the carved decoration projecting in relief above the surface.

The armoire illustrated, of about 1800 to 1820, is carved with a scrolled and medallion lower skirt, a vine the full height of the central style, and shell rosettes and whimsical figures on the upper frieze. All are in sharp relief, projecting well above their surrounding surfaces, and completely original under several layers of overpainting that has not been stripped. Three armoires are known with this carving pattern, all by the same maker. *Royal Ontario Museum*

Fig. 17: Quebec is the fakery centre of Canada, where upgrading or adulteration of genuine antique pieces is virtually a cottage industry. With furniture, the great majority of early pine cabinet pieces, such as armoires and buffets, had their original paint stripped – often with scalping of surface wood as well – during the great naked-pine fashion of the 1950s to 1970s. That was just the beginning.

This two-tiered pine buffet of about 1770 to 1790 (opposite), once painted an ochre red, is a good and genuine early piece, with raised end panels that originally had plain surfaces and Louis xv-shaped door panels. The carving is all recently added embellishment, upgrading fakery. Original carving on such pieces always stood in relief, as on the preceding armoire (Fig. 16).

On this buffet, the carving is intaglio; it has been scored and chiselled down into the original surfaces, rather than relief carved. With rare exceptions, however, intaglio or incised carving, as opposed to relief carving (Fig. 16), was not a feature of original eighteenth-century Quebec furniture. The decorative carving on this buffet is all a recent addition, including that on the side panels and frame, and the interwoven wreaths and the rosettes of the door panels. The scalloped skirt is another embellishment, an added strip under the originally straight skirt.

The added intaglio carving type of upgrading is very common on originally plainer Quebec furniture. All of it is the work of carver-fakers, of variable skill and proficiency, and all done within roughly the past forty years. *Royal Ontario Museum*

Fig. 17a: Looked at in detail, the intaglio carving of the door panels of the two-tiered buffet (Fig. 17) is both flush with the panel surfaces and, like that in Figure 10, less than skilfully done. Though the buffet was originally painted an ochre red, it was completely stripped in the early 1960s. Since the added carving shows no traces of the earlier paint, the carving was clearly done after the piece was stripped. *Royal Ontario Museum*

Fig. 18: This low armoire is another good example of the Quebec fakers' penchant for carved decorative upgrading. In its basics, the armoire, with its raised Louis xv door panels and plain raised end panels, is a quite genuine late-eighteenth-century piece. In the late 1950s, its original paint was then totally stripped. Following that, in the late 1950s or early 1960s, the armoire then acquired its grooved end-panel shaping and the shallow intaglio-carved floral decorations in the door panels and drawer fronts. The carving is crude, hardly up to eighteenth-century standards, but still better than the incompetently carved medallions on Figure 10.

In that state, stripped of paint and now including its fake decorative carving, the armoire was illustrated in Jean Palardy's *The Early Furniture of French Canada*, 1963, no. 143. Following that, but before 1966, the armoire then reacquired its "original" finish, a blue-green stain-paint, carefully applied with a soft cloth. Thus, this piece, in its stripping, carving, and later repainting, has seen the hand of at least two different upgrading fakers. *Royal Ontario Museum*

Fig. 19: Not all embellishments that are later added to much older pieces are necessarily fakery in an antiquarian sense. In the nineteenth century, with its plethora of styles, furniture was occasionally updated by its own owner-users, changed or decorated in some way to bring it closer to what was then a modern fashion. In the same manner, early furniture today is often reupholstered with contemporary fabrics, possibly with modern patterns quite different from any possible original upholstery.

Intaglio thin-line carving in a pseudo-Eastlake style has been added to this Quebec maple Louis XIII chair of the early eighteenth century. The carving was done not by a dealer or upgrading faker, but by the then-owner in the late nineteenth century, in an attempt to bring a Louis XIII chair more into the fashionable Eastlake style of the 1870s and 1880s. *Private collection* the lower section could quickly become a single-unit low buffet, or *buffet bas*. The upper section, with added short legs, front and side skirts, and a change from the upper cornice to a flat-surfaced top, could also become a second small and quite credible *buffet bas*. Thus, the possibilities for furniture alterations, marriages, and divorces are limited only by imagination and the materials available.

Married pieces are usually furniture, but not always. In Montreal one summer years ago I had occasion to go into the shop of the then-single-largest dealer in early Quebec antiques. The shop was known, I must say, for some pretty dubious practices, including brutal stripping and refinishing and the "improvement" and "upgrading" – otherwise faking – of a lot of furniture.

The owner-proprietor, normally a tough old guy, knew me. He usually sat at his working desk right inside the front door, keeping an eye on both his customers and the cash drawer. As I went in, the poor man was sitting there, holding part of a silver church chalice, and totally in tears. He was sobbing as if his dog had just been run over.

As he gradually calmed down, it emerged that he had bought the chalice ten minutes earlier. It had simply walked in off the street. The dealer had taken one quick look, seen a good early Quebec punch-mark on the base, and instantly shucked out a thousand dollars, cash. Cheap, for a maker-marked $3,000 chalice, even at that time. The chalice might have been stolen, of course, with the seller fencing it as burglary loot, but at that price I'm not sure the dealer was overly concerned. I doubt he even asked how the unknown seller had come by it.

Quebec silver church chalices are four-piece assemblies. First is a base, into which the lower end of the stem is threaded and screwed. The upper stem is then internally threaded to take the screw-in bowl, which is often fitted into a separate outside decorative cup.

The chalice was all disassembled, and its four parts were lying on the dealer's desk. Dripping tears, he pushed the pieces towards me. The base included very nice acanthus-leaf *repoussé* decorations and, on the underside, a very genuine-looking *Marion* stamp of Solomon Marion (Montreal, — 1782–1832 —). The stem had no maker's mark, though stems usually don't, and at the bottom it looked as if the threading had been freshly recut. Indeed it had, to screw into the somewhat different threading of the base. The threading of the bowl base had also been recut, to fit the stem-top threads. The bowl and outside cup likewise had no maker's stamp, though they often do. The cast decoration of the outer cup did not remotely match the *repoussé* acanthus leaves of the base, though on genuine pieces they always do.

The dealer, who had then been in the business for over forty years and who, of all people, should have known better, had bought himself a married piece, a faked-together chalice assembled from parts of either two or three other chalices. Presented with a bargain too good to resist, he'd jumped at the deal before really looking at the chalice, rather than after. Then he'd cracked up when his own greed backfired. Well, anyway, he had a possibly genuine Solomon Marion-marked base. Who knows, given some of the quiet silver-faking talents around, perhaps the bowl later acquired a Marion mark and a new decorative outer cup that matched the base.

Dealers often employ independent refinishers and cabinetmakers to do their restoration, repairs, and refinishing – and their alterations and upgrading fakery, including marriages and divorces. Thus, many severely altered pieces are not amateurish or crudely done at all, but are very carefully matched and blended by professional cabinetmakers. Some marriages, divorces, and upgradings, where the cabinetmaker also knows how to "antique" his alterations and blend finishes, can be difficult to identify precisely and may escape discovery for a very long time.

Compared to single-unit furniture such as desks or buffets, original two-sectioned Canadian pieces are much less common, and even rare in some forms. Consequently, they are likely to be high-priced, and often well worth the effort and work of alteration and marrying. Since fakers have already launched decades of work into the market, prospective buyers should be particularly on the lookout for married or divorced pieces. Any piece of two-sectioned Canadian furniture should be examined doubly carefully, in extreme detail. Like Quebec church silver, two-sectioned cupboards or secretary-desks (Figs. 14, 15) are particularly likely to have experienced substantial alteration, either divorce or marriage. Any bookcase, cupboard, or buffet that appears as if it might have once been an upper or lower section of a two-sectioned piece should be turned upside down and checked for signs that a new base and legs or a new top may have been added.

Beyond even married or divorced pieces come miscellaneous assemblies, or pieces wholly "made-up" from miscellaneous parts. Made-up miscellaneous assemblies occur most often with furniture (Fig. 15). The first requisite for the faker is a supply of reasonably matching old wood and a good store of bits and pieces of long-broken or partial early furniture, as well as of old lumber. Parts, usually recut and reshaped to fit new furniture forms, can come from any number of partial or unrestorable original pieces. In Canada, made-up pieces are typically pine cupboards, cabinets, or, most commonly, "harvest" tables, but only rarely more formal hardwood furniture.

Made-up furniture typically shows some variation in the colour of wood and the finishing of the various components. Thus, those signs of a faker's work are usually concealed either by complete stripping and refinishing or by reproduced "original" paint. Usually a made-up piece is easy enough to spot, simply because something, or several things, about it just seem funny or wrong. The problem is to figure out just what is wrong. Usually one can conclude that a piece is totally unreal or made up only after a thorough examination of every part and every construction detail.

I have occasionally met dealers, mostly in shops that focused on overly refinished country furniture, including upgraded pieces and even reproductions, who actually got rather touchy if a customer looked at pieces too closely, perhaps knowing some of their offerings could not quite stand the full light of day.

In one exchange where I had the good sense to keep my mouth shut, I was with my wife in a shop; we were alone except for the dealer. I was wandering, opening drawers and cupboard doors, and looking finally at a small single-door Quebec pine low buffet with "original" blue paint. The eighteenth-century lozenge-carved panelled door looked as if it might perhaps be genuine, though I never got the chance to really examine it. The rest of the piece clearly looked new, with wood of standard modern widths for one-by-four and one-by-six lumber, apparently made up just to take that particular door. I could even see knots – unknown in early pine furniture – under the rather thin paint. It was not a Quebec buffet construction that I had ever seen.

I guess I was lingering over the made-up buffet too long for the dealer's comfort. He finally sort of snarled from the front of the shop, "What are you doing?" "Just looking," I responded. "Oh," he called, in a quite testy manner, "I thought you were taking measurements!" As we ceased looking and left, his parting comment was "That buffet's my best piece. Good investment piece for someone." "Yea and verily," I responded as we exited, leaving him to figure it out. The message is that any time a dealer clearly does not want a piece examined too closely, or gets touchy about it, head for the door.

There are grey areas between what constitutes marrying or divorce, making up, and extensive restoration, for the same piece can combine elements of all three. Marrying of two or more components, of course, is outright fakery, as is fitting and assembly of bits and parts into something different from any previous original piece. Just where the dividing line lies between deceptive fakery and honest restoration is also difficult to define.

Restoration involves the stabilizing or repair of an otherwise original and genuine piece, as well as any necessary replacement of missing segments. Restoration, however, does not imply changes to style and design or to shape and construction. The question of the extent of restoration or reconstruction that is acceptable before a piece enters the realm of miscellaneous assembly as a made-up fake is a matter both of the nature of the piece being restored and of personal opinion. There is no rigid rule.

Normally, restoration, including replacements, of 20 to 25 per cent of an original piece is considered about the maximum, while 50-percent restoration, including replacement of major components, would be at least partial fakery. A greater degree of restoration of a very rare or fine piece would perhaps be more acceptable than of a very common piece. There are, however, all sorts of shadings of what may be acceptable in each circumstance, and every restoration or replacement decision presents an economic and ethical judgement call. Paintings, particularly, sometimes get restored to the point that there is more restoration than original painting. They are still accepted as genuine, but often discounted in value as too heavily restored.

Many pieces, especially furniture, that get severely battered or have numerous or important parts missing may not be worth restoring. The costs of the restoration work may be more than the piece would be worth restored. If restoration does not make economic sense, the piece becomes a "junker" or, in British parlance, a "breaker." It goes into a dealer's barn or storeroom until a need arises for its wood or some parts for marrying, divorcing, or making up into some other piece.

In saying that every extensive restoration calls for sometimes contradictory considerations, let me try a hypothetical scenario. Suppose the Thomas Nisbet drop-leaf table (Figs. 5, 5a) had been found "in the rough," badly broken at some point. One side drop-leaf, two of the four legs, and the end drawer are all missing and lost. Almost 60 to 70 per cent of the original table is still intact. From its unmistakable details we know it is (or was) a Nisbet table, though the label has long since separated from the underside of the top, leaving only an obvious lighter-coloured rectangle where the label certainly once was.

Since there are still existing parts to serve as patterns, the missing drop-leaf and legs can be duplicated and replaced, though at some considerable cost. The missing drawer is a problem, since we don't know whether its front had a beaded edge or what kind of hardware it had. So, we make up a drawer according to what we think the original must have been. Finally, since we know the table once had a Nisbet label, we make up a counterfeit (Fig. 20) and apply it over the discoloured rectangle.

So, what do we wind up with: a fake, a partial fake, a made-up miscellaneous assembly, just an extensive 30- to 40-per-cent restoration to approximately original form, or all – or which – of the above? This is also an expensive job, so let's say the new rope-twist legs, the drop-leaf,

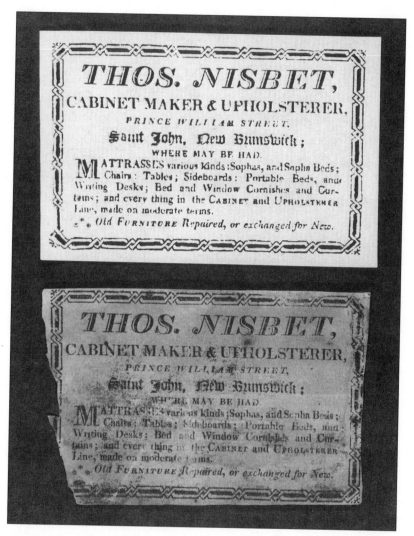

Fig. 20: Fake labels have not yet shown up, or at least been discovered, on Canadian furniture, though they have in Britain and the United States. As an experiment and a purely academic exercise, we started with a photograph of a Thomas Nisbet label of the 1820s (Fig. 5a). Then, with some creative photocopying on rag paper (top illustration), followed by some creative aging, we emerged with a fake or counterfeit label (bottom), ready to paste on a genuine but anonymous piece of early New Brunswick mahogany furniture. This label, however, while it has the appearance of age, does not show the deterioration of age, and thus would not pass close inspection. *Author files*

the drawer, the counterfeit label, and careful refinishing will cost perhaps $4,000 to $5,000. We also know that the value of this table, even all back together, will not approach the value of a similar all-original Nisbet table, though in appearance it *will be* an original Nisbet table.

Should the table, given its losses and damage, even be restored at all, or will the end result be worth the cost? Instead, should the table perhaps be left as a breaker, for its remaining parts to be applied to some other broken table? Conversely, should some other broken table be found for parts of old wood that can be reshaped and included in this table? If it is offered for sale, how should it be described? I will now leave this ethical and financial dilemma to the reader.

Though they are not fakes in the sense of being created to deceive, some quantity of recently imported European pine furniture also falls into the fake category because of fictional attributions. Just as considerable English-Canadian furniture over many years has been shipped to the United States and has taken on American nationality, so has a considerable quantity of European and American furniture and other objects come to Canada (Fig. 21). Dealers import European formal furniture by the container-load, and though much of it may be nineteenth- or early-twentieth-century reproduction, it is still usually sold as what it is, of English, French, Italian, or whatever origin. That is not necessarily the case, however, with English and European pine country furniture.

The most widespread pine of Britain and Western Europe, from Sweden and Norway to northern Spain, is the Scots or Baltic pine, *Pinus sylvestris*. Scots pine in Europe was as commonly used for simpler furniture as was our White pine, *Pinus strobus*, in North America. Much nineteenth-century European pine furniture was also quite similar in form, style, and construction to English- or French-derived Canadian and American furniture. Large quantities of this European pine furniture have been imported during the last three decades, and some now appears in the market as Canadian, attributed to Maritimes, Quebec, or Ontario origins.

Canadian-attributed European pine furniture does not seem to be

Fig. 21: This pair of eighteenth-century panel-backed "Louis xiii" chairs is typical of European pine furniture masquerading in the market as Canadian. The Louis xiii style was, in fact, less a style in the modern sense than a generic post-medieval furniture type. It was prevalent and universal throughout Britain and Europe until the coming of "designer" styles in the late seventeenth century.

These chairs were imported as part of a dealer's cargo some time in the 1950s or 1960s, and then circulated in the antiques market as "Quebec, Louis xiii, early 18th century." Since the "sausage" stretcher turnings and panelled upper (rather than lower) backs are rather anomalous for Quebec-origin Louis xiii furniture, someone finally got curious. Sure enough, a wood-cell examination (Chapter 5) showed the wood to be European Scots or Baltic pine, not native to North America at that time. A little regional style and design research concluded that the chairs are probably Swedish. The last time the chairs were sold, it was for what they are, perfectly genuine probably Swedish chairs of the early or mid-eighteenth century.

These chairs appear to be an example of someone's wishful belief, in this case that all pine furniture *must* be Canadian, which is hardly the case. Beneficial mis-attributions (or deliberate fiction) can stay with antiques through many changes of hands and, in the absence of suspicion or curiosity, perhaps never be discovered. *Royal Ontario Museum* overly common yet, since most pieces are sold as what they are. There may, however, be much more mis-attribution than we are aware of. In many cases, too, mis-attribution of origin has probably happened accidentally and simply has not yet been discovered. Dealers and collectors alike also share a broad assumption that *any* pine furniture has to be Canadian, which is hardly the case. Since the values of European antique furniture are as high as those of Canadian, however, and for finer pieces even higher, there seems little or no financial gain in deliberately applying fake country-of-origin attributions. Still, European would-be Canadian furniture is very much in the antiques market, and is very confusing. More on this is covered in Chapter 5.

Counterfeit furniture labels have not yet appeared, or at least have not yet been discovered, on Canadian furniture. Perhaps this is because there are so few known early labelled pieces, no more than perhaps three hundred made before 1840. Virtually all of those are now in museums or private collections, to the point that only a collector's financial distress or death is likely to bring one on the market. Thus, a label faker in Canada would probably have difficulty getting access to an original label for copying.

Only four Canadian cabinetmakers before the 1850s are known to have labelled their furniture. The most noted is Thomas Nisbet of Saint John, New Brunswick, with nearly two hundred labelled pieces of the period 1814 to 1834 now identified (Fig. 5a). The short-lived partnership of Tulles, Pallister, and McDonald of Halifax is known for just three labels of 1810 to 1811, and John Tulles alone for one other from 1812 to 1826. Daniel Green of Saint John is known for only two surviving labels, one on a large mahogany dining table of about 1820 to 1825. In contrast, many American cabinetmakers of that same period used labels, and numbers of American counterfeit labels have been discovered.

Label faking is very difficult. The difficulty lies not so much in counterfeiting the label (Fig. 20), but in getting it to pass close inspection. Paper labels a century or more old, and pasted or glued to wood, have been subject to long-term light exposure, to great temperature and humidity variations, and to the influence of the tannic acid present in all woods. These conditions are very destructive to paper, even early rag paper. Thus, genuine paper labels are not only darkened and stained by age and light exposure, but they are also usually weakened, often to the point of being brittle and flaky or partially desiccated. Museums now often carefully lift labels for preservation, de-acidifying them and keeping them separately in acid-free Mylar envelopes. Giving a faked label the flaked-away or acid-rotted look of having been pasted on a piece of furniture for many decades, however, would be virtually impossible.

Fake labels have usually been placed on pieces of previously unlabelled and anonymous furniture. Since no previous label has covered the wood beneath, however, and hindered age discolouring, the wood under a fake and recently applied label will be the same age-darkened colour as the surrounding wood, rather than lighter. Thus, peeling back or lifting a label will provide an obvious clue to whether it was recently applied.

Beyond making a counterfeit label appear ravaged with the real desiccation of true age comes the problem of placing it on exactly the right piece of furniture, perhaps a reason why label faking is not often attempted. The furniture, like silver or any other object, would itself have to be genuine and of the same time period, style, and workmanship as other known pieces by the labelling maker, altogether a difficult proposition. Even if the label itself passed inspection, if it was on a piece of furniture that differed in any way in date or style, or from other known work by the same maker, it would still be discovered as fake.

Large quantities of European or Asian blacksmith-made decorative ironwork now circulate as Canadian in the antiques market, most of it also recently imported. These iron objects include the fat lamps called "betty," or "crusie," lamps, various candleholders, window grills and small gates, fireplace cooking tools, such as forks, tongs, fire grills, spatulas, and decorative hardware, such as door hinges and latches, as well as many other items. Most seems to be of French, Spanish, or Asian origin, and much appears to be recently made and artificially corroded and blackened, true and deliberate fakes.

This iron seems to acquire Canadian nationality quite readily, and anything appearing even remotely French in style quickly becomes "Quebec, eighteenthth century." Iron is impossible to date just as a material: dating can be done only stylistically or from archaeological contexts. I suspect, particularly, that the majority of iron "betty" lamps on the market are European and that most of them are recent fakes.

I once saw a large cardboard carton full of just such "betty" lamps, of black iron, newly imported from Spain and still to be rusted, in the trunk of a dealer's car. They were essentially perfect, all handmade by blacksmiths and yet virtually identical, dozens nested tightly together in that carton. The importer-dealer admitted to me that he was going to "antique" the lamps by burying them for six months in a sand pile mixed with road salt and kept wet. What a road-salt-and-sand mixture does to cars it also does to fake ironwork. When the lamps were rusted, perhaps pitted, and certainly "antiqued," the dealer was then going to "float" them into antiques shows and flea markets. The one thing he did not admit was his certain intention to let them become genuine and original early Canadian lamps.

Good blacksmith-made black-iron tools, such as brush hooks, garden hoes, grain sickles, and very French fur-trade-looking hatchets, are sold in every public market in Mexico. Iron fur-trade hatchets and pipe-tomahawks are also being reproduced in the United States. There are still plenty of blacksmiths around the world, particularly in countries with low labour costs, who are quite capable of making, or reproducing, anything in the area of antique ironwork.

With iron, there is really no way to judge either age or, with universal and generic forms and blacksmithing methods, the country of origin. Thus, the many collectors of decorative ironwork also have to presume that a lot of "early Canadian hand-forged iron" on the market is recent European or Asian fake. Modern reproductions are also part of this problem, including pieces, marked or more usually unmarked, made and sold in the blacksmith shops of restored historical-village museums.

Just as with makers' punch-marks on silver, makers' names – or, more particularly, engraved inscriptions – on iron, steel, or brass improve values and thus should also be treated with a healthy dose of suspicion. Makers' marks on tools or on iron and steel housewares are almost always genuine, simply because antique tools and implements have not generally reached the price levels at which fake marks are worth the effort or could substantially raise values. Makers' names were also typically stamped or rolled, with steel stamps, into tool steel while the metal was red hot. Adequately faking stamped makers' marks would involve both proper fake stamps and the reheating of early tools, a proposition not worth the cost and effort.

Engraved inscriptions are something else. Enough bogus or doubtful inscriptions have emerged on otherwise genuine iron, steel, and brass pieces (Figs. 22–24) to make any inscription of a presentation or name, or a place or date, at least initially questionable and worth serious examination with a good magnifier. If the names or events in the engraving are well known or historically significant, the inscriptions should be taken as doubly dubious. Iron and steel were not common choices for presentations and inscriptions, *except* for firearms and swords, which were often engraved as gifts. Silver, however, was always preferred.

Beyond engraving or inscriptions on metals, engraving on bone, ivory, or whale tooth – so-called scrimshaw – must automatically be suspect. Just as with Indian trade silver or ironwork, the market is so flooded with fakes that all engraved scrimshaw should be presumed to be fake until it can be established otherwise. During long weeks at sea, bored nineteenth-century sailors, both on whaling ships and other vessels, often carved decorations on sperm-whale teeth and whale bone. The scenes were as varied as the individual carvers, and many are known from the Canadian Arctic, which were mostly done by whalers. Though once fairly common, in recent years original scrimshaw, as a form of folk art, has become scarce and increasingly expensive. Reproductions, becoming fakes, have taken over that market.

Fig. 22: Virtually all antiques in metal seem to be potential candidates for fake inscriptions. This sword includes such a blatant and crude example of engraving that it should never have fooled anyone. The blade bears, on the upper right side, an inscription in mixed lettering "Souvenir de montcalm." The inscription does not indicate that the sword was Montcalm's own, or from the Battle of Quebec in 1759. In the mid-1950s, however, based apparently on nothing but hopeful supposition or self-delusion, it was first acquired by a well-known Quebec dealer and then sold to a very discriminating private collector. The otherwise quite genuine but plain brass-and-bone-hilted sword is probably German, of the 1800-to-1815 period. The Montcalm inscription is totally spurious, and was done probably in the 1940s or early 1950s. *Royal Ontario Museum*

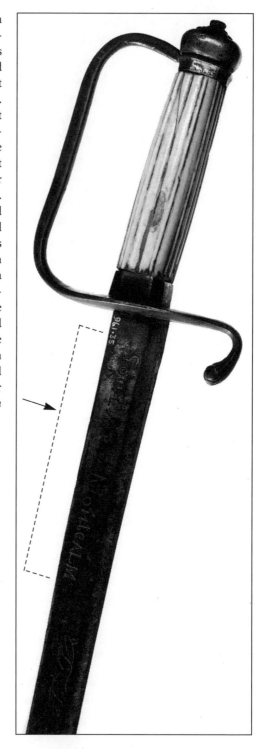

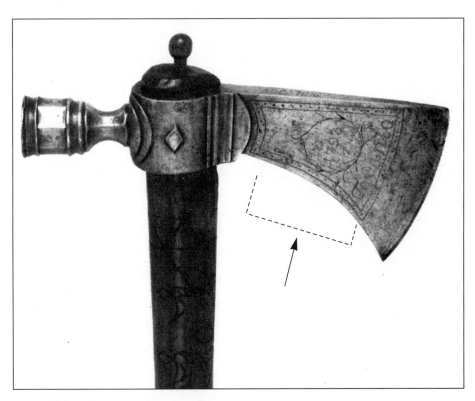

Fig. 23: Fake Canadian inscriptions on Indian pipe-tomahawks appeared in the 1980s, with an apparent English origin, but aimed at a North American market. This iron tomahawk is probably original, but could equally be an artificially corroded recent reproduction. Iron is easy to age artificially, complete with rust scale and corrosion pitting. The piece is inscribed to Lt. Charles Duke, 26th Reg't., Toranto (sic), 1793, in script that does not match that time period. Present-day Toronto was in fact founded as York in 1793 and renamed Toronto only in 1834. The first local regiment was John Graves Simcoe's Queen's Rangers, or 1st American Reg't. The very shallow inscription also appears to have been added over older rust pitting. This piece sold at an international auction house in London in 1989.

Two other pipe-tomahawks with similar spurious Toronto inscriptions, and identical in form, are also now known. One is inscribed "To Capt. J. Parr" and "From Wm. Claus," with "Toronto 1793" on top of the blade. That piece sold at an auction in New York for $4,675 in 1985. A third piece, also with engravings and an inscription "Toronto 1793," was offered to the Toronto Historical Board in the mid-1980s, but was declined as a probable fake.

Numbers of other engraved pipe-tomahawks are known, most with American inscriptions, and a good percentage are no doubt fake. *Author files*

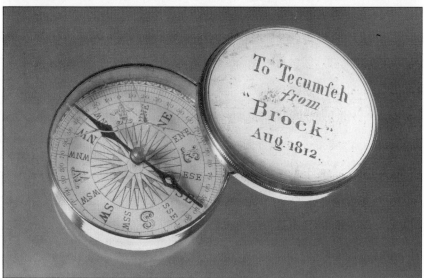

Figs. 24, 24a: The Brock compasses pose a mystery, for one of the two illustrated here is clearly a fake – not as an object, but as a presentation piece. Early in the War of 1812, the lieutenant-governor of Upper Canada, General Isaac Brock, led British reinforcements to Fort Malden, arriving there on August 13, 1812. He then joined with Ohio Shawnee chief Tecumseh for the successful capture of Detroit on August 16.

In gratitude following the victory, Brock supposedly gave his ally Tecumseh his brass pocket-compass (just one), which is supposedly the piece illustrated as Figure 24 (top). Tecumseh's lieutenant, Chief John Naudee, according to an old written provenance with the piece, then had the compass lid engraved in Detroit soon after Tecumseh was killed at the Battle of Moraviantown on October 5, 1813. This would have been impossible. The British had evacuated Detroit a week earlier, on September 27, and no British-allied Indian would have been present in Detroit after that.

The small brass-cased pocket compass, as an instrument, is consistent with the War of 1812 period. The script engraving "6th Aug. 1812" is also consistent with the period, but erroneous, and possibly a mistake for 16 August. The engraving "To Tecumseh / Fort Detroit / Frome / "Brock" was done much later, probably after 1900, and is spurious. The strange mixture of lettering styles, the mix of upper- and lower-case letters, the misspelling of "from," and the name "Brock" placed in quotation marks all point to an inept forgery, as well as much later engraving. The script engraving, which is probably genuine, is much more worn than the later inscription, but the actual significance of the "6th Aug. 1812" remains unknown.

The other Brock compass, in Figure 24a (bottom), is more likely the genuine gift to Tecumseh. The compass itself is perfectly consistent with the War of 1812 period, as is the lettering and style of the engraving. The lid was probably engraved shortly after Tecumseh's death, though certainly not in Detroit.

There are a number of other engraved presentations to Tecumseh known to exist, not only of the compasses, but of tomahawks and trade silver as well. Since it seems unlikely Tecumseh had multiple gifts showered upon him, any Tecumseh presentation inscription should be treated with some suspicion. *Royal Ontario Museum*

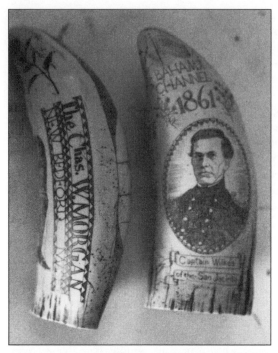

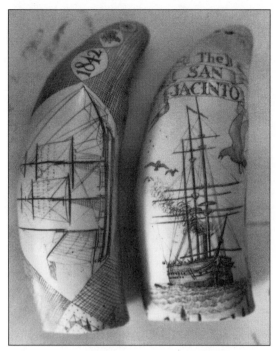

Figs. 25, 25a: Fake scrimshaw, of carved scenes or motifs on whale tooth, bone, or tusk, has flooded the antiques market in recent years. Most of the fakes seem to be English-manufactured and of newly made-up scenes, in the style of, but not copies of, genuine nineteenth-century pieces. There are also, however, a handful of museum-licensed reproductions of pieces in museum collections. The material is a polymer plastic, and the engraving, though very realistic, is mechanically pressed and then hand-finished.

These two scrimshaws of American vessels, one of the whaler *Charles W. Morgan* (Fig. 25), dated 1861, and the other of the *San Jacinto* (Fig. 25a), dated 1842, were acquired by a Canadian collector in Spain. Over three-hundred fake scrimshaw scenes and decorations have been identified so far, including Canadian arctic scenes. Since fake scrimshaw in the antiques market now far outnumbers genuine pieces, it has taken on the name "fakeshaw." *Private collection*

A few years ago a woman called me about checking two pieces of whale-tooth scrimshaw (Fig. 25), which she had acquired on a trip to England. By courier, she sent them to the museum for checking. One was of the famous whaling ship *Charles W. Morgan*, dated 1861. Both looked "wrong," and both failed the hot-needle test (described in Chapter 5). The *Morgan* still exists, and I called Mystic Seaport, the huge maritime museum at Mystic, Connecticut, where the vessel is a great attraction. I learned that Mystic Seaport gets two or three calls a week about scrimshaw, virtually always fake, and that there is no known original version of the *Morgan* scrimshaw. It is a wholly made-up fake.

During the week that I had the two fake scrimshaw pieces, I got yet another call about another *Charles W. Morgan* piece. The caller had bought this one in Spain, and he faxed to me copies of photographs. The *Morgan* scrimshaw in his photographs, and the piece on my desk, were identical to the last detail. Neither caller was particularly upset to learn their pieces were fakes, for a lot of calls to museums are from people who already suspect what they may hear.

Fake scrimshaw, now called "fakeshaw," began entering the market in the early 1970s – all of English origin and most from a single man-ufacturer. The fakes are made of a polymer plastic that closely matches the texture and age patina of genuine tusk, tooth, and bone. The engraving is mechanically impressed and then scribed and coloured in by hand. Except for a few authorized reproductions from museum collections, the scenes are fictional, not copies of known original scrimshaw pieces. The technology of polymer plastics has made pos-sible production of fake bone and tusk that visually and by touch is difficult to tell from the real thing.

Unfortunately, not just with silver, iron, or furniture, but with other antiques that are simple pieces, or that are relatively easy to fake or upgrade by people who know what they are doing, it is not always pos-sible to determine absolutely that something is a fake or has been faked. Sometimes the best an examiner can do is "reasonably establish" doubt or say that the "balance of probabilities" suggests a fake or upgrading (or that a piece is probably genuine). Rather than absolute certainty, we thus come down to the legal term of "beyond a reasonable doubt."

Though probably 90 per cent of Canadian fakes or faked pieces have something about them that ultimately gives them away, ultimately can be a very long time, perhaps years or decades after a fake first comes on the market. No expert is immune from mistakes. Authors have many times illustrated pieces, which they presumed to be genuine, that later turned out to be fakes. Perfectly genuine pieces have sometimes been denounced as fakes. Totally fake pieces, such as LaMontagne's "Great Brewster Chair" (Fig. 13), have also been affirmed and reaffirmed as genuine. For this reason, any "experts" who consider their opinions or judgements as infallible are simply indulging in egocentric self-delusion. No "expert" is infallible.

For fakers, of course, particularly those who are superb craftsmen or as expert as the "experts," that is good news. They may not be able to fool everyone all of the time, but if they can fool enough people much of the time, that is sufficient. Thus, to extend the old art-world saying, that "in the name of Art you can get away with anything," the same is most certainly true of the antiques world and markets. Remember, *caveat emptor.*

4

FutureFakes:
The Problems of Reproductions

"No humbug is great without truth at the bottom, for the true meaning of humbug is to take an old truth and put it in an attractive form."
– Phineas Taylor Barnum, 1856

Despite all the books that have been written on fakes, and the forty or fifty years during which Canadian fakes have accumulated in the antiques market, in recent years reproductions have emerged as an equal but much more rapidly growing problem. Reproductions, like any other commodity, are very much market-driven. North American home-renovation tastes and decorating practices – aided, abetted, and promoted by a plethora of glossy mass-market magazines full of articles, advice, and colourful audience-targeted advertising – have spawned a huge demand for historical design and antique decor in home furnishing.

Even beyond that hype and push, however, rapid cultural change, including our ever-faster pace and our increasingly complex technological society, seems to have created something of a backlash. Makers of reproductions have perceived a strong popular urge for a return to the simpler past, for a return to an age of greater cultural stability. Whether that simpler, more-stable past was ever a reality, North American home decorating has beyond doubt gone on a great nostalgia kick. As a result, since genuine antiques, by any definition and of any form, are an ever-diminishing commodity, and often show signs of age and wear as well, the growing demand has long since led to extensive reproduction of objects from the past.

A reproduction, by definition, is a modern, recent, or, at least, later copy or replica of some earlier object that is no longer made or manufactured. Reproductions, in the first instance and by their original makers, are sold for just what they are, and usually, though not always, at prices below the antiquarian values of similar and original antique pieces.

Pure economics, in fact, governs the production of reproductions. Anything that becomes popular or fashionable – remembering that the ultimate goal of advertising is to make things desirable – also often comes into widespread demand. Virtually any obsolete or antique object, for which demand exists or can be created, and where something can be produced and sold for less (or sometimes even more) than antique prices for the same object, is a candidate for reproduction. Thus, the motivation for reproductions is the same as for fakery: capitalizing on market scarcity and demand. The only question is whether the reproduction is done purely, perhaps with considerable handwork, or as a mass-produced adaptation from some original version.

The exception to reproductions underpricing antiques lies mainly with objects that are reproduced for active or hard use, where safety or durability may be a concern. Here, genuine antiques, even repaired and restored, may still be too worn or weakened and too fragile for continuing use. In this active-use category, horse-drawn buggies, buckboards, and sleighs are all now being reproduced, wholly new, at prices very considerably higher than those for surviving nineteenth- or early-twentieth-century antique versions. The same is true for cast-iron wood-burning kitchen cooking stoves, which have never gone totally out of production. These are being reproduced by several American foundries, and one in Canada, at much higher prices than even restored original stoves. Reproduction wooden mahogany or cedar-strip boats, both the sleek inboards of the 1930s Chris Craft type and outboard-motor boats as well, are being made once again, and are expensive. Handmade wooden cedar-strip canoes are back in fashion, at five times the price of moulded fibreglass canoes. In these cases, reproductions have simply filled the market niches for nostalgia-oriented buyers where genuine antiques that once took stress, weight, or heat are no longer suitable for continuing active use.

Reproductions may be precisely exact copies of genuine pieces that were used as models, but are not necessarily so. Many reproductions, to allow for efficiency of fabrication or large-scale manufacturing, are instead design adaptations from original versions. Adaptations can include changes of materials, construction methods, and details, and of decorating, assembly and finishing techniques, all to suit more mechanized and cost-efficient methods of production.

Reproductions have come about, particularly during the last thirty to forty years, because of the huge increase in antiques and collecting since the Second World War. Antiques collecting in the post-First World War era of the 1920s and 1930s was still a rather elitist pastime, centred mostly in New England and the middle South, and was severely limited by the Great Depression. The first American specialized antiques magazine, *Antiques!*, was founded as recently as 1922.

By the later 1940s, however, the popularity of collecting began to expand, heavily inspired by new fashions, home-decorating magazines, and the formation of historical-village museums. Since Canada, in fashion and design, has always been strongly influenced by American trends, the historical-decor and antiques media hype in everything from magazines and films to recreated historical villages (often used as film locations) had an impact here as well.

Original antiques are irrefutably a limited and non-renewable resource. Once an object becomes antique, by any of the several definitions, there is simply no more of it being produced – at least in original versions. The natural attrition of time, wear, discarding, or destruction, inexorably and inevitably, is gradually reducing the surviving supply of that object.

Ever-increasing collector demand in the face of ever-declining supplies not only creates higher prices for whatever supplies remain, but the higher prices also create economic opportunities for the production of reproductions. A great many fashion- and decor-oriented people want the superficial image of good antique furniture, silver, ceramics, or whatever. Far fewer want to make the effort to observe, read, and learn about antiques, or spend the time visiting dealers or attending auctions and antiques shows to find antiques, or spend the money to acquire, restore, and maintain antiques. Thus, this large decor-focused market reads decorating magazines such as the American *Country Homes*, *Country Life*, *Early American Life*, or the Canadian *Century Homes*. The decor-oriented population then turns to buying reproductions, making that also a sizeable market, and supporting a large though fragmented reproductions industry.

There is considerable rationale for home-furnishing with reproductions. The collecting and keeping of antiques – whether furniture, pictures, or silver, or specialized and dedicated collections such as coins, stamps, glass, ceramics, or ancient swords and daggers – involves liabilities as well as pleasures. The true collector is by definition also a curator – and must be – simply to safeguard the collection and preserve the investment in it. He or she can never really own antiques, but only serve as their custodians. Properly cared for, antique objects can and do long outlast mere people, who are only their transient possessors.

To maintain and preserve a collection, the serious collector takes on heavy responsibilities and costs. Theft- and fire-resistant housing are requisites, with the appropriate alarm systems. For high-value organic materials such as antique furniture or anything else of wood, paper, or fabric, temperature and humidity control is essential. No collector needs furniture veneers loosening from extreme dryness or leather rare-book bindings developing mould or mildew from summer humidity. For pictures, particularly prints and watercolours on paper, light-exposure control is also critical. Pictures cannot be hung in bright or directly sunlit rooms, lest they discolour and fade. For valuable collections of small objects, insurers may insist on fireproof safes or built-in vaults. All of this necessary infrastructure is expensive, and, on top of it, there are always ongoing collection or fine-art insurance premiums.

A real question, considering the collections as well as the investments in preservation and security, is whether true collectors as custodians *pro tem* really own their collections or whether their collections own them. It does not matter whether the collections are of high-value fine art or rare 1930s cone-topped beer cans. Collectors, particularly specialized collectors, can become obsessed, with both their personalities and lifestyles dictated by their collections.

Many people, however historically or fashionably antique decor-oriented they may be, simply do not want to live or be tied down as the custodians of high-value objects, the way dairy or beef farmers are the prisoners of their cattle. They want the image of historical and antique furnishings, but not the constant attention and care, the expensive infrastructure, or the special insurance costs that the real thing entails. Perhaps they have a home where undisciplined kids, untrained pets, careless cleaning help, less than sober dinner guests, or any and all, may pose a constant threat to a high-value antiques collection. Perhaps they want to be comfortable about taking off for two February weeks to the Caribbean without having to hire house-sitters or worry constantly about fire or burglars. Perhaps they just don't want to give serious financial investments quite the exposure to risk they would encounter as home furnishings, always hoping the guests will use the coasters and ashtrays.

I have a plain but quite genuine raised-panel early-nineteenth-century Quebec armoire, which I use as a supplies cupboard in my home office. This is perhaps now a $3,000 to $4,000 piece that I bought thirty-five years ago (in the rough, dirt-cheap, followed by a month's work). It sits there, doesn't make conversation when I'm working, and I don't worry about it. The idea, conversely, of having a highly carved Quebec Louis XV $50,000 or $100,000 armoire as my office-supplies cupboard, or a $250,000 American chest-on-chest in my dining room, I would find more than a little scary.

Contemporary lifestyles and family economic priorities, as well as hype and advertising, are probably equally as strong motivators for the

huge reproductions market as is the ever-more-limited availability
and rising cost factor of genuine antiques. In the narrower realm of
collector-antiquarians and the antiques market, however, some reproductions have become very much a problem, and others will in years
to come.

The basic trouble with all reproductions, and particularly very exact
copies, is that, following their initial manufacture and marketing, their
makers lose any control over where they go or what may happen to
them. Most reproductions, at least honest reproductions, are marked
by their makers to advertise and spread the brand name and to avoid
confusion with earlier and original versions. The markings may be
either a relief or intaglio (impressed) brand name included in the
casting mould for iron or glass, an indelible stamp or even a hot brand-
ing for furniture and wood, and punched or stamped markings for
silver or brass. Most makers of reproductions do make some attempt
to prevent their products from getting into the antiques market and
being treated and sold as genuine pieces.

Still, as a reproduction travels through subsequent owners, usages,
sales, and perhaps changes, there is no maker's mark yet devised that
is impossible to blot out, erase, grind off, fill in, scrape and polish away,
or remove by whatever clever method a faker might devise. Beyond
their first sale, reproductions can be altered, have their maker markings removed or changed, be artificially aged, get refinished, and easily
be misrepresented in future sales. The jump from reproduction to
"antique" is an easy one, particularly in an unsophisticated market.
Thus, many reproductions can very easily become fakes – and, unfortunately, a great many do (Figs. 26–28).

One good example of this was much of the huge English ceramics
industry throughout the nineteenth century. During this time it was
reproducing older English patterns and styles, and reproductions of
Chinese porcelains (Fig. 29) and of Continental delft and faience.
German and French porcelain factories as well were reproducing
earlier and obsolete patterns, some equal in quality to the original
eighteenth-century types, but many not. It is probably safe to say that
every form of high-quality English, European, or Chinese ceramics

Fig. 26: Many reproductions, even though they may bear only a superficial resemblance to early or original styles, still commonly get into the antiques market as genuine pieces. Quebec eighteenth-century *os de mouton* chairs invariably had legs and stretchers that were hand-carved and roughly round or oval in cross-section. The legs and stretchers of this chair were cut with a band saw, and are rectangular in cross-section. Thus, only the basic shape of the stretchers even remotely resembles the earlier Quebec chairs. Still, this chair was sold by an antiques dealer, and bought by a collector, as a genuine eighteenth-century Quebec piece, some twenty-five years ago.

The reproduction chair frame is actually Italian-made, and is a factory-made adaptation rather than a precise reproduction of the French late-Louis XIII *os de mouton* style that was also fashionable in eighteenth-century Quebec. This chair pattern is still available, and as a reproduction has been sold as an unfinished and unupholstered frame, for completion by the buyer. Some years ago I saw several of these chair frames, newly imported and of bare fresh wood, in a Quebec antiques dealer's workshop. I have sometimes wondered what became of them. *Private collection*

Fig. 27: As a new piece, this birch stool, in an eighteenth-century Louis XIII form, was made by an independent cabinetmaker in the 1920s or 1930s, before the present age of reproductions. The turnings are incorrect for the early eighteenth century. Rather than being intended as a deliberate fake, however, this stool was more likely made as a replacement or as a reasonable copy of another piece. As with so many older reproductions, and particularly individual cabinetmaker creations, the stool did eventually wind up in the antiques market and was subsequently sold as a genuine eighteenth-century stool. *Royal Ontario Museum*

Fig. 28: This ladder-back chair is another piece that should never have entered the antiques market. The salamander back slats and French down-curved arms indicate Quebec origin, but that is about all. The chair appears to be a late-nineteenth- or early-twentieth-century-style revival piece. The form is derivative, though not an accurate reproduction, of eighteenth-and early-nineteenth-century New England ladder-back types. In its tall, multi-slatted back, the chair may instead have been inspired by the widely publicized Wallace Nutting "Colonial" reproductions of the 1920s. The motive behind the chair, whether it was made as a reproduction or a deliberate fake (not a very good one), is unknown. In any event, it circulated for years in the Quebec antiques market as an eighteenth-century Louis XIII chair. *Royal Ontario Museum*

Fig. 29: Not all reproductions are recent, or financially motivated. Sir Alexander Mackenzie (1764–1820), the famous fur trader and explorer to the Arctic and Pacific oceans in the 1790s, returned to England from 1799 to 1802. While there, he ordered, through the East India Company, a full dinner service of Chinese porcelain, to be decorated with his family crest. On his return to Montreal in 1802, he brought the dinner service with him. When he retired and returned to Scotland in 1812, he gave the dinner service to his cousin Roderick McKenzie (different spelling) in Montreal.

After two or three generations of occasional breakage, in the 1860s the McKenzie descendants in Montreal had some of the porcelain copied and replaced – this time in England. Thus, the service now consists of both the original 1800-to-1802 Chinese pieces and the 1860s English reproduction replacements.

The Chinese dessert plate on the left has a slightly blueish tone and uneven surface, while the 1860s English reproduction on the right is both whiter and smoother-surfaced. *Royal Ontario Museum*

Fig. 30: Copying or reproduction is hardly a recent phenomenon; it has been practised whenever and wherever markets existed. Ontario nineteenth-century potters were an ingenious group, making miniatures and special pieces, as well as copying imported English forms that were popular at the time. Slip-casting became a simple technique of small Ontario potteries for making pattern pieces that could not be turned on a wheel. Plaster of Paris, applied to any existing piece of pottery and then cut free in sections, could provide a mould for slip-casting reproductions.

The small pitcher on the left is English, of white earthenware, from the 1840s or 1850s. The pattern, in moulded relief, is of foliage and flying birds. The piece on the right is an Ontario potter's slip-cast copy, of the 1870s or 1880s. The Ontario pitcher was cast from a plaster mould made from the English white pitcher or its duplicate. The clay is a red-firing rather than a white earthenware, and the finish is a lead glaze over brown slip. Taking a plaster mould from an existing piece of pottery always means a loss of detail in the pattern of the copy pieces, as is the case here. The Ontario potter's piece is also slightly smaller than its pattern pitcher, from shrinkage during firing.

Both pieces are antique, just through age, and the Ontario piece is also a reproduction, though hardly a fake. *Royal Ontario Museum*

Fig. 31: Canadian nineteenth-century redware pottery can be reproduced, but would be difficult to fake. The plate on the left was made by William Eby (1831–1905) in the 1870s at his pottery near Conestogo, Ontario. Eby dug his raw clay from the banks of the Conestogo River, and fired his lead-glazed pottery in a wood-fuelled kiln with extremely variable temperatures. The end products emerged with inconsistent colour of both pottery body and glaze. The Royal Ontario Museum reproduction, on the right, is of modern, purified clay and glaze and was fired in an electric kiln with very precise temperature control. A true faker of the same plates would have to go back to the old method: digging natural clay, using a lead glaze, and building a wood-fired updraft kiln. The reproduction plate, new and with an impressed ROM marking, would be hard to mistake for an original Eby plate. With some actual use, wear, and possible chips, however, and the ROM mark ground out, twenty or thirty years hence this plate may still take its place in antiques shows. *Royal Ontario Museum*

produced before 1850 has been reproduced since, and sometimes by several different makers at different times.

As early as 1909, the American Consulate in Edinburgh warned the U.S. State Department that great quantities of "antique" ceramics and furniture that were even then being exported from Britain to the United States were reproductions or outright fakes (Appendix One). English and European ceramics reproduction, some of it very, very good, continues right to the present. Both a factory in China and another in Taiwan are even today reproducing Ming dynasty (fifteenth-century) blue-on-white porcelain.

Fortunately, Canada has so far been spared widespread reproduction or fakery of Canadian ceramics, largely because, until the 1870s, the Canadian ceramics industry produced only earthenware utility wares. Until recently antique pottery values were too low to encourage faking or reproduction, and the few attempts at true fakery (Fig. 8a) are little more than jokes. The Royal Ontario Museum and several other museums, however, do offer a few well-marked Canadian earthenware reproductions (Fig. 31) for sale. Many eastern American museums also sell a great variety of reproduction American pottery, both redware and stoneware, and a number of independent potters make a wide range, some on contract to museum shops.

Assuming the eventual wear-and-tear of age and usage, the only real point of separation between a reproduction and a fake is the question of commercial intent. Was a piece originally made, or manufactured, for initial sale from new materials and with a modern finish, as well as an honest description, and does it have a reasonably indelible maker's marking of what it is? In that event, it is a true reproduction, either a copy or replica of some original piece that was used as a model or a new piece patterned on or adapted from a particular design or style.

If, however, the reproduction was either altered after it left its initial maker and marketer or was later used or sold as original, with an intent to deceive or defraud the buyer, then it immediately becomes a fake (Figs. 26–28). Intent has always been a key to the definition. Given the inadequate product knowledge of many dealers, however, the offering of a reproduction as genuine can easily be inadvertent if the dealer cannot tell reproduction from real. Thus, a reproduction, though originally perhaps quite honestly made to be sold as a reproduction, after gaining some natural distress of age and passing through a few hands, can easily become a fake even without intent, just in the way it is offered and sold.

For example, hundreds of thousands of pieces of nineteenth-century and early-twentieth-century English reproduction furniture, made during the Chippendale and Georgian revival of the 1860s to 1920s, have wound up in North America and have now taken on the cachet of genuine eighteenth-century pieces. Herbert Cescinsky made the point, as early as 1931 in his book, *The Gentle Art of Faking Furniture*, that the wealthier and upper-class population of mid-eighteenth-century Britain included fewer than 140,000 families. That number, Cescinsky felt, with only a small percentage actually furnishing houses at any time, could not even have begun to commission from cabinet-makers or use the massive quantity of supposedly "eighteenth-century" English mahogany furniture that, as early as the 1920s, had been exported to the United States.

The U.S. Department of Commerce in 1935 issued a warning that at least 75 per cent of the "antique" English furniture coming into the country at that time was reproduction or fake. Charles Hayward, later the author of *Antique or Fake*, had himself apprenticed before the First World War as a cabinetmaker in a large English fake-furniture shop. English "Georgian-period" furniture has kept coming ever since, today by the container-load. The supply seems endless. Thus, Cescinsky may well be right, and the great majority of English "eighteenth-century" furniture now gracing North American homes and antique shops may, in fact, be later-nineteenth and early-twentieth-century reproductions.

Though they were not as faithfully copied from the original furniture as were the English reproductions, and though they have some manufacturing adaptations such as dowelled joints, a wave of Federal-style furniture reproductions accompanied and followed the

American Centennial of 1876. Reproduction American Colonial and Federal furniture has been manufactured in great quantity ever since, to the point that "colonial" is now a generic furniture advertising term. Some of these nineteenth-century reproductions, now antique in their own right with well over a century of usage, aging, and mellowing – and perhaps more recent restoration or refinishing as well – at least visually can easily appear to be genuine eighteenth-century pieces.

A reproduction, initially made and sold as such, once it has gained the status of age and a cachet of originality, can at one and the same time be both a fake and an antique. With the mass-manufacturing of reproductions of virtually anything economically worth reproducing over the last forty years or so, the problems of defining and distinguishing can only grow worse. In fact, the individual faker, a skilled and meticulous artisan in the handcrafting of some objects, may slowly be driven out of the market by new materials, technologies, and the full-out mass-production of antiques reproductions virtually identical to the originals.

As many later-nineteenth- and early-twentieth-century factory-manufactured objects have become scarcer with time, they are now both accepted as "antiques" (Definition-3) or as "collectibles," that dreadful catch-all term, and are highly fashionable. With the declining availability of original manufactured objects, their corresponding antique prices have increased from the level of just second-hand furniture or discarded household objects to equal or exceed present-day manufacturing costs. That sort of an economic disparity has created an open invitation for reproductions to enter the market, as they have in vast quantity.

In the current market, we have to separate reproductions into two categories, mass-produced commercial reproductions and individually made or "museum" reproductions produced in much more limited quantities.

Commercial reproductions, which by now include reproductions of almost anything fifty years old or more, and sometimes not even that, are made in quantities limited only by the numbers that can be sold before they saturate the market. Very often these pieces are actually adaptations from early forms, patterned on basic designs, rather than exact replicas of original objects (Figs. 26, 32, 33). Advertising of commercial reproductions is a mainstay of decorating and home-decor magazines. As well as being marketed through furniture dealers and interior decorators, many reproductions are also offered through glossy universal-distribution catalogues.

"Museum" and individually made reproductions are a wholly different breed. Usually either exact replicas of pieces in museum collections, or based on them, museum reproductions are sold mainly in museum gift shops or specialty boutiques or catalogue outlets under a museum name. Typically these reproductions are limited to smaller objects, since they are mostly sold in small shop spaces. The objects, then, are produced by contracted fabricators in small quantity, often no more than a few hundred at a time. Museum and boutique shops do not like to carry large inventories. Attention to detail is meticulous, and the reproduction prototypes often have to be approved by museum curators or very knowledgeable special committees before they go into production. Museum reproductions can be reordered and kept in stock for years, but very often, too, the immediate market is exhausted with a single reproduction order. Thus, when the initial inventory is gone, that reproduction is dropped and replaced with another.

In large operations, such as Colonial Williamsburg's catalogue-sales branch, marketing is carried on continent-wide through a large catalogue rather than from a single museum shop. Williamsburg licenses their fabricators for Williamsburg Reproductions and allows some to market in their own right as well as becoming sole suppliers to Williamsburg. Some items, which sell in reasonable volume, and continuously, may be carried for decades without change.

In our twentieth-century throw-away age, objects tend to have very short life spans – much shorter than in the pre-industrial era. Then they are gone, either succeeded by newer models or just replaced entirely by more advanced forms. Where are mechanical portable typewriters in an age of laptop computers? Where are 1920s and 1930s wooden-cabinet radios, crank telephones, or 1940s round-screen televisions? Where are wooden-handled kitchen utensils, ceramic and coloured-glass kitchen bowls, or tinned-copper pots and pans? Where are glass milk bottles or Coca-Cola bottles with the labels moulded in relief instead of decaled on. Where are cast-iron hand-push reel lawnmowers or brace-and-bit drills among tools, or wooden fish, cheese, liquor, or butter boxes as containers? All of these and many other once-common objects are gone, extinct, becoming antique under the Definition-3 category of things no longer being produced. The surviving original objects, of course, eventually wind up in antiques shops and shows.

A generation or two later, with many objects that have simply become obsolete, a nostalgia market develops, and with it the demand that generates reproductions. Wooden-handled kitchen utensils and coloured-glass mixing bowls are back, as are cast-iron coin banks and sheet-metal toys. So are wooden radio cabinets, but with modern radios inside, and oak ice-boxes, now made to hold TVs or "entertainment centres." Leaded-glass "Tiffany" lampshades and electric ceiling fans, after decades out of fashion, are again very much "in." Even five-cent-Coke-bottle machines, 1940s Wurlitzer "juke boxes," and mechanical five-cent slot machines, or "one-armed-bandits," are again being produced for recreation rooms with a nostalgic flavour.

Though it may be surprising since we think they are also gone, many other objects, though long obsolete, have always retained enough residual demand to remain in continuous though small-scale production through the decades since they were in common use. Among these "living antiques" are glass-and-metal "railroad" kerosene lamps, cast-iron baking utensils, blue-and-white-enamelled pots and pans, mechanical apple-parers and cherry-pitters, cast-iron hand-cranked meat grinders and spice graters, hand-cranked coffee-mills, small cast-iron kitchen water pumps, pottery mixing bowls, hand-scrubbing washboards, brass hand or school bells, and hand butter-churns, to name just a few. Most of these old standbys are sold only through catalogues and specialty stores. Still, in the present age of historical nostalgia, between continuously manufactured old standbys and newer reproductions, one could totally stock a full "antiques" shop from catalogues alone.

Fig. 32: Reproduction chairs, as revivals of virtually every antique style and form, are now being made by dozens of furniture factories and independent cabinet-makers throughout Canada and the United States. Some of these are nearly exact copies of eighteenth-century cabinetmakers' pieces, while others are copies of later factory-manufactured chairs.

The English Chippendale style, of the mid- and late eighteenth century, is one favourite for reproductions, and has been for well over a century. Thus, far more late-nineteenth and early-twentieth-century reproduction English and American furniture is now in the antiques market than was ever produced as originals in the eighteenth century.

The chair on the left is a genuine and quite rare Canadian piece, a mahogany Chippendale chair with a separate upholstered slip seat, made in Montreal in the 1790s. The more elaborate piece on the right is a new and unfinished Chippendale reproduction. Like Figure 26, the chair frame is Italian, imported as loose parts, for assembly, finishing, and seat-frame upholstery in Toronto. This reproduction can never be confused with an original piece, for both its mechanized manufacturing and method of assembly is quite obvious in anything more than a superficial glance. *Royal Ontario Museum*

Fig. 32a: The reproduction Chippendale chair (Fig. 32, right) can never be confused with a genuine example, for the construction is quite different. The reproduction chair is assembled, as are most reproductions, with dowelled joints (Figs. 40, 41), while original chairs and most other pre-1870s furniture had mortise-and-tenon joints. The seat frames of the two chairs are also different. The original chair (left) has simply a rabbeted groove on the seat-frame inner edges, to hold the separate upholstered slip seat. The reproduction chair has the same rabbeting, but the entire frame also has three slots on the inside, to take a fingered corner brace on each corner. This is a mechanized adaptation never seen on an original chair. The carved moulding below the seat front is a separate applied strip, while on an original chair any carved decoration would be integral with the seat frame.

Most modern reproduction furniture shows fairly obvious mechanized fabrication and assembly differences that would make it difficult to confuse with genuine antique pieces. This is not necessarily true, however, of many older or nineteenth-century reproductions. *Royal Ontario Museum*

The advent of very similar or identical manufactured reproductions, or the increased production of old standbys, also has a tendency to cap the antique value of older original objects at about the same level as the reproductions. Beyond that, much of the potential market for the antique versions, in classic economic substitution, simply moves to the modern reproductions. Given two similar or virtually identical factory-manufactured objects, one sixty years to a century old and one new – if antique quality and rarity factors is not an issue – a great many people will not pay an antique price premium for age alone.

In this area of manufactured reproductions, we now have such widely reproduced items as brass beds, pressed-wood or pressed-back chairs (Fig. 33), Windsor chairs, most oak "Arts and Crafts" and "Mission" furniture, pine "country" furniture, vast quantities of pressed and moulded glass (Fig. 37), and cast iron in all forms, from firebacks to toys and coin banks to oil-lamp or flowerpot wall brackets (Fig. 36). Carefully crafted and exact "museum" reproductions, sold mainly in museum gift shops and specialty boutiques, add many more exotic and esoteric objects.

One good example of the way in which reproductions restrain antique values is evident in the case of pressed-back chairs (Fig. 33, left). These were made by dozens of North American factories from about 1890 to after the First World War. Though hardly rare, pressed-back chairs are now somewhat scarce in good condition or in original four-to-eight-chair sets. The Eaton's and Sears-Roebuck catalogues in the early 1900s offered these chairs for roughly a dollar each, but by the late 1970s and early 1980s, when they were being sold as antiques, the asking price had reached around $100 to $150 each – or somewhat more for identical chairs in sets of four or six.

Then came reproductions, from several makers. Reproduction pressed-back chairs, almost identical to the originals and made right in Toronto, are now selling for under $100 unfinished and are available in any quantity. Original early 1900s-period chairs have not advanced in asking prices or matched inflation since the early 1980s, when reproductions first appeared. Original pressed-back chairs can still be found, even restored and refinished, for around $120 to $150, and sometimes less. Reproductions have simply capped the prices of the originals.

For another good example, late-Victorian and early-twentieth-century brass beds have enjoyed a resurgence of fashion over the past twenty years. Original 1900s brass beds, and particularly more elaborate models, are relatively scarce. Out of fashion by the 1930s, many disappeared into Second World War scrap-metal drives. (Second World War scrap-metal collections, in great patriotic fervour, swept away vast quantities of earlier objects in copper and brass, iron and steel, and aluminum.) Normally a heavy fashion-driven demand would drive up the prices of a commodity in such limited supply. Early brass beds in the antiques market reached roughly $400 to $500 by the late 1970s, coinciding with the arrival of the first newly manufactured reproductions. Since then, original and antique models, overwhelmed by the supply of reproductions, have not really advanced much in value. With rising materials and manufacturing costs, in fact, the prices of new reproductions have risen instead, so that today original antique brass beds can often be found for less than half the price of new reproductions.

Only if a craft-period piece is extremely rare, fine, elegant, or maker-marked does the appearance of reproductions not depress or cap the value of a surviving antique, and virtually negate the investment and capital-gain potential. The effect is equivalent to a company issuing thousands of shares of new stock, which, without added value, such as the acquisition of another company or the building of new factories, simply dilutes the value of its outstanding shares. Thus, any other than the rarest and finest of antiques, where earlier reproductions exist or are in current production (or may even come in the future), are not exactly good investment or capital-gain prospects.

To sum up what the examples show, the appearance of quantities of reproductions almost immediately undercuts and limits antiques market values and prices for the same objects. To many decor-oriented people, however, the appearance and image of home decorating with reproductions is as satisfying as having the antiques themselves, and often much less expensive. However, antiquarians, since some newly

Fig. 33: A great variety of reproduction pressed-wood or pressed-back chairs are among the forms that, with a little age and wear, could easily be mistaken as originals. Original chairs of this type are hardly rare and are still readily available, but reproductions are also being made by at least eight North American factories, all with sizeable production. The original chair on the left, a manufactured piece of oak, dates from about 1910. The chair on the right, unfinished, is a new reproduction, also of oak, made in Toronto. Neither is maker-marked. These are both factory-manufactured chairs, and, except for the use of more-efficient 1990s machinery, the manufacturing methods for both chairs are very similar. *Royal Ontario Museum*

Fig. 33a: The wooden seats of both pressed-back chairs are glue-laminated, the only difference being a retaining strip inserted in the seat front edge of the earlier chair, but unnecessary in the reproduction. Contemporary adhesives are far superior to 1900s glues. After the disappearance of most old-growth forest by the 1860s, and with it the availability of very wide lumber, the seats of all plank-seated chairs such as Windsors were of edge-laminated strips rather than single wide planks. With the same variety of patterns, the same wood, the same manufacturing methods, and here even the same Robertson screws (introduced in 1908) for the seat-to-back braces, contemporary reproduction pressed-back chairs are essentially identical to the early 1900s pressed-back chairs. *Royal Ontario Museum*

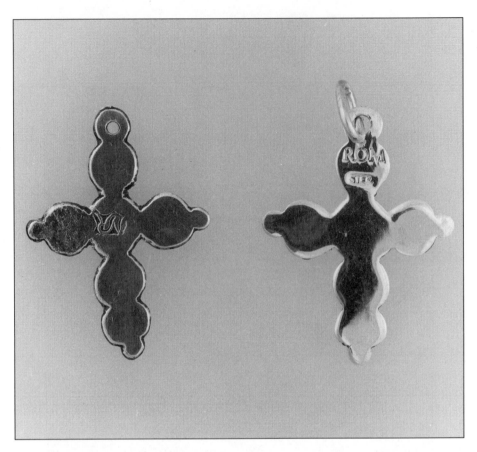

Fig. 34: Tiny trade-silver crosses, about one inch (2.5 cm.) high, were made in quantity by Narcisse Roy of Montreal (1765–1814) and several other Montreal and Quebec City makers for the North West Company. As the example on the left shows, the original crosses were stamped with Roy's script NR punch-mark. The Royal Ontario Museum has since reproduced the cross, shown on the right, and stamped the reproductions with a ROM logo at the top. It is very unlikely, with the indelible stamping, that the ROM reproduction could be confused with or sold as an original piece, nor would a small silver cross be worth enough to justify the effort of altering the punch-marks. *Royal Ontario Museum*

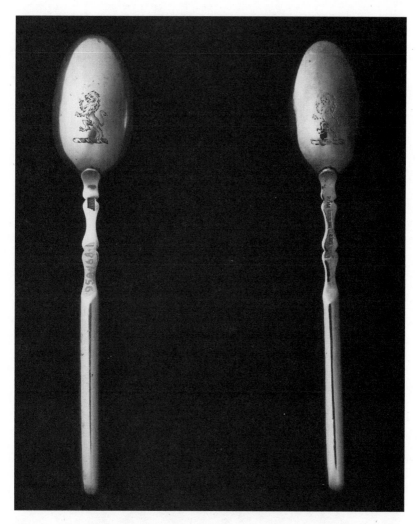

Fig. 35: Antique silver flatware has been reproduced by a number of Canadian and American museums, using pieces in their own collections as patterns. This combination teaspoon and marrow spoon was reproduced by the Royal Ontario Museum. The genuine piece, on the left, has a badly worn IS mark of Jacques Varin dit Latour (1736–1791) of Montreal. The reproduction, on the right, has a ROM mark, a STERLING mark, and the modern punch of the silversmith who reproduced the spoons. Though the three punches in the reproduction spoon could conceivably be infilled with sterling-silver solder, with a passable colour match, a new punch-mark of Varin dit Latour or of another eighteenth-century Quebec maker would have to be added. The present values of early Canadian flatware (as opposed to elaborate church or table silver) are not yet high enough to justify that effort, though in the future the market may be different. *Royal Ontario Museum*

Fig. 36: Canadian cast iron appears in many forms. This iron wreath (top) of maple leaves and a recumbent beaver was probably a decorative appliqué for a stovepipe cover. It was cast in Ontario in the mid-nineteenth century, but is unmarked, so the foundry remains unknown.

The Royal Ontario Museum commissioned a reproduction (bottom) for sale in the museum shop. The pieces are identical, except that the reproduction has four short legs on the reverse side, for use as a trivet. The reproduction is also unmarked. If the trivet legs were ground off, and some accelerated rusting done, the reproduction could easily acquire enough patina of old brown corrosion within six months to pass as genuine in the antiques market. *Royal Ontario Museum*

manufactured reproductions are nearly identical to the older, manufactured "antique" versions, fear that the separation of antique from
reproduction is going to pose real identification problems and
headaches a few decades down the road.

I never cease to be amazed – after many years of examining other
people's finds, treasures, purchases, bargains, mistakes, and disasters
– at the human capacity for self-delusion, blind belief, or plain dumb
self-confidence on subjects of which they are totally ignorant. To quote
the old saying: "A little knowledge is a dangerous thing." Much of this,
of course, is caused by greed or the will to believe. Firm belief that
grandmother's maybe-1880s dinner plates are in fact the last surviving
cargo of the *Mayflower* makes them more valuable in one's own mind.
Beyond that, once beliefs or delusions have solidly rooted, it can be sur-
prisingly difficult to get through with sense and reality.

In spite of the vast quantity of fakery and reproduction out there,
there are still people who approach the antiques market with complete
self-assurance but little knowledge, really negligently. On the outer
fringe of self-delusion, in my experience, are often the people who take
speculative wild flyers, impetuously buying something in a way that
they would never even consider when buying a hundred shares of
stock or a used car. Once later doubts develop, as they very often do,
many of these misadventures wind up being brought to museum curators for another opinion.

A memorable visitor one morning was a bit unusual to begin with,
mid-forties perhaps, unshaven, with dirty clothes, long, stringy hair,
and worn-out workboots. At least he'd made an appointment, rather
than just appearing as a walk-in. Day to day, we never knew who was
likely to emerge, or with what objects, and I learned long ago not to
judge identification visitors just by dress.

"Hank," of no last name, carried with him, as he'd said buoyantly
on the phone, an uncut mint-condition sheet of four Island of
Newfoundland 1850 one-pound notes. As he took it out of a green
plastic garbage bag, I saw that the sheet was framed rather than loose.

This made the paper and printing a bit harder – but hardly impossible – to examine.

As Hank pulled his treasure from its bag, it just looked wrong, even from across the room. The printing was only in black on white paper, with no colours. The paper the bills were printed on was also too white and clean; the condition was just too perfect.

"I paid six hunnerd bucks for this," he started in. "It catalogues at five hunnerd just for a single bill, so it looked too good to pass up."

"Do you collect early paper currency?" I asked him.

"Nope," he said, "but I got this Charlton coin and money catalogue, see, and I was at this here flea market, and there it was. This guy had it with a lotta other stuff. I go through old stuff at all the flea markets an' keep my eyes peeled for good deals. Kind of a hobby. I checked in my catalogue, an' I beat the guy down from nine hunnerd he was asking. Like I say, it was too good to pass up. A real steal, eh?"

"So why'd you bring it here?" I asked.

"Because my old lady's givin' me all kinds of heavy static about it. She thinks I blew six hunnerd bucks on somethin' I don't know nothin' about, and maybe I got myself screwed. She wanted somebody in the museum to look at it."

"So, let's have a closer look," I said.

He passed over the framed sheet of bills. I took my ten-power magnifying glass from my desk drawer, laid the frame flat, and put the magnifier down on the glass.

The diagnosis was obvious, instantly. I wish every identification were this easy. I could clearly see the fine screened grid of photolithograph printing, a screen of perhaps 140 to the inch (2.5 cm). The bills had been copied from the steel- or copper-plate engraved printing of all early paper currency, but reproduced by the wrong method on the wrong paper. This sheet of four rare Newfoundland one-pound bills was a reasonable copy, but still a modern reproduction, printed probably in some quantity. In its frame, I couldn't really look at the paper, but it certainly wasn't anything like nineteenth-century rag-based currency paper. My identification visitor had indeed "got screwed."

I tried to let Hank down gently, but I had to tell him his great bargain was a modern reproduction. He was totally incredulous. He couldn't believe it. He wouldn't believe it. So, I had him look at the printing himself through the magnifier. He could see the tiny dots. Then I plucked a book off my shelves and had him look at a high-quality colour illustration through the magnifier. He saw the same screened grid and tiny printed dots. The day's *Globe and Mail* was on a chair. I had him look at a front-page photograph, with its somewhat coarser-printed grid for newsprint paper.

It all finally came together in his mind, and he looked totally sheepish. I told him he'd bought a modern reproduction, not a true fake. With its screened-grid rather than line printing, and unstained and unfaded white paper, this sheet of bills didn't show an attempt at real fakery. No one had even tried to make it look genuine.

"So, what can I do?" he almost begged. "My wife'll have my balls off." I doubted quite that, though of course I didn't know his wife.

"All you can do is go back to the flea market where you got this and try to find whomever you bought it from. Then try to return it and get your money back. Tell him I said it's a reproduction. Maybe he knew that, or maybe he thought it was genuine, too. I don't know. If he fudges or says no, your only other option is to try to sue him in small claims court. Still, you have to admit that you jumped into this without knowing what you were buying."

Hank had no response to that, except desperation. "So, what's it worth, say even bein' a copy? It's *gotta* be *worth somethin'!*"

Though I do perhaps hundreds of identifications every year, museum policy is that we leave value appraisals to dealers and auction houses. In this case, however, I had to tell him. "Maybe the price of the frame, but the notes have no collector value. Unless you can manage to return it, I'm afraid you're stuck."

In the end, I couldn't save him. All I could do was let Hank sadly re-bag his "deal" that was "too good to pass up" and go back to the tender mercies of his wife.

As Hank's story illustrates, the problem of reproductions being mis-identified, misinterpreted, or deliberately offered and bought as antique and genuine (Figs. 26–28) is not just a problem for the future.

It is very much a here-and-now problem, and a very rapidly growing problem. The whole great game of antiques collecting is one of wits as well as knowledge, with everyone seeking advantage. Buyers are out for bargains and sellers are after the top dollar. With no laws or regulations requiring seller disclosures, unlike those mandated for stock prospectuses or now even for used-car histories, it is little wonder that provenances get invented and the truth often gets a bit bent.

Following the P. T. Barnum dictum, there seems to be no way of protecting the ignorant or foolish from themselves. As genuine and unimproved antiques have become more scarce, and finer pieces have all but disappeared from the market, dealers have had increasing difficulty not in selling but in buying and in maintaining a full inventory of desirable pieces. The once commonly available supply of nineteenth-century, much less eighteenth-century, antiques is rapidly drying up. Thus, reproductions, both new and old, have gradually crept into the antiques market and increasingly inhabit many antiques shops and shows.

The upper-level dealers and larger urban antiques shows are pretty scrupulous, for they have to be. Those shows are usually organized by volunteer groups or clubs for charitable purposes rather than for organizer profits. They also often have dealers' booths and exhibits vetted by knowledgeable committees, to try to catch faked pieces or "antiqued" reproductions sneaking in. The upper-level dealers themselves, often with established clientele and reputations to defend, would no more dare publicly to exhibit a reproduction than they would a known fake.

No more than 10 per cent of dealers or antiques shows, however, are in that upper-level league. The other 90 per cent, many small and often part-time rural dealers and localized shows run by profit-motivated promoters, are considerably looser. These shows are typically not vetted, and some are difficult to tell from flea markets, where just about anything goes. In small antiques shops as well, reproductions are mixed together with genuine pieces. After visiting a great many such shops over the years, I now fully expect to find at least one or two reproductions mixed in with other pieces, and usually do.

The reproductions seem to get into the antiques market either inadvertently, because the dealers themselves are unaware, or deliberately.

Even though they know the pieces are reproductions, the dealers think they will make a good mix or balance with the rest of their inventory. Sometimes, the reproductions will be tagged and offered as reproductions. Other times, reproductions, like everything else in a shop, will have no descriptions, but just their price tags, leaving the customers to figure it out for themselves.

On other occasions and in other shops, real game-playing predominates. It appears that, like at least some of the dealers, a large proportion of the generalist collectors simply do not know and cannot distinguish the differences between the real and unreal. Sometimes the objects have price tags but sometimes not, in which case you are expected to ask the dealer. The price quoted then depends on your appearance, or the car you were seen getting out of, or perhaps just the dealer's estimation of your fiscal health.

Very often, too, the sales technique is either silence or unrelated prattling by the dealer. In most shops with a mix of the real, the faked, and reproductions, rather than giving fraudulent and self-incriminating sales pitches, the dealer is likely to remain quiet and just let pieces sell themselves and customers make their own judgements. The mere fact, of course, of a reproduction being displayed in an *antiques* shop at all gives it a certain banner of authenticity, and if the customer doesn't know what he or she is looking at, why, *caveat emptor*, that's their problem. The dealer can be faulted only for offering false information, not for silence or idle chatter.

Most reproductions on the market today are made of new materials with modern finishes and are initially marketed as reproductions. Most are easy to spot, usually because of design adaptations or construction methods, and will take decades of use and wear actually to appear antique, if they ever can. Some individual cabinetmakers, however, in both Canada and the United States are now producing very accurate reproduction furniture of old wood. Old wood, particularly wide pine planks, can often be found stacked away in rural barns. Hardwoods suitable for turning such things as bedposts or table legs can come from old beams or even from long-dead but still-standing trees.

Making reproductions from old wood is not a viable proposition for factories, which require large and reliable supplies. The old-wood supply is sporadic and usually found in small quantities, and takes hunting down, a bit here and there. For individual cabinetmakers who scour the countryside for limited-quantity material, however, it is a worthwhile endeavour. Using old wood and pre-industrial construction techniques to achieve the realistic aged appearance of an antique improves the sale prices of their products.

Unfortunately, accurately constructed old-wood reproductions can be very difficult to spot precisely, since they are quite real in every sense but age. By definition, they are actually fakes advertised and sold as reproductions, with no fraud initially intended. Unlike most factory-produced reproductions, many old-wood cabinetmaker reproductions also have the capacity to enter the antiques market virtually the day after they are produced and successfully pass as antiques perhaps forever more.

In saying that present-day reproductions, down the road a few decades, are going to present real problems of detection and identification, I may be understating the case. In looking at Canadian dealers and antiques shops today, only the upper-level still sticks to selling antiques by the more stringent Definition-1. Though it may be a dying idealism, these dealers maintain some qualitative standards, and thus remain the suppliers to the most demanding and purist market, however small it may be.

The vast majority of antiques shops either already are, or are fast becoming, glorified flea markets on one hand or combination Definition-3 antiques, reproduction, and gift and boutique shops on the other. In the average Canadian antiques shop today, I would venture that probably not more than 5 or 10 per cent of the offerings now predate 1900, and much is from the 1920s to the early 1960s. These are, however, still Definition-3 antiques. Virtually everything that can be collected is being collected or at least acquired – by someone. Thus, many antiques shops try to offer virtually everything, from old automobile oil cans to Prince Charles and Diana commemorative wedding china to iron railroad weigh scales or block-ice tongs to bottles by the thousands.

While dictionaries may define words one way, people may also be well ahead of dictionary compilers, or Canada Customs. The term "antique" has very clearly changed over the past few decades, from Definition-1, meaning age alone, to Definition-3, meaning probably no longer being produced. Given the extreme popularity of collecting, we cannot criticize this. Not everyone can afford, in terms of finances or custodianship responsibility, to collect $5,000 to $20,000 Canadian silver or $20,000 to $50,000 Canadian furniture. Not everyone wants to, for obvious reasons.

Likewise, in our throw-away age of quick obsolescence, even simple objects that were once common can largely disappear and achieve scarcity in a very short time, and thus become candidates for reproduction. I have both a son and a nephew who collect and have hundreds of beer cans, of which a few 1930s cone-topped versions have now been reproduced. Common children's sheet-metal toy cars, trucks, and airplanes of the 1930s and 1940s, worn out or rusted, have been discarded to the point that they are now scarce. Thus, many are also now being reproduced. Some toy companies have even reintroduced and are again marketing fifty-year-old models. Dolls, from pre-First World War porcelain-headed cloth dolls to plastic Barbies with all their accessories, are being reproduced in far greater quantity than original versions ever were. Thousands of poster subjects, including virtually every known movie poster, wartime recruiting poster, or Picasso exhibition poster, have been reproduced. So have sheet-metal signs, beer trays, and all manner of advertising memorabilia.

Collectors of late-nineteenth- and early-twentieth-century glass, particularly, are faced with a massive quantity of reproduction. In Canadian glass, many maker attributions, particularly to Mallorytown or Burlington, are suspect to begin with. Early blown glass – and some patterns of pressed glass – was made by more than one company, including many American companies. Thus, many glass patterns hopefully attributed as Canadian may well not be. Beyond that, many forms of glass – including milk glass, "Depression" glass, cranberry glass, carnival and satin glass, Canadian and American pressed glass, Tiffany glass, and certainly others – have all been reproduced (Fig. 37). The reproductions are often nearly identical to the original forms, and in

Fig. 37: Collectors of glass have to contend with a plethora of reproductions, as well as uncertain attributions. Among many pressed-glass patterns, produced in numerous forms from kerosene lamps to goblets to dinner plates, is the Canadian "Rayed Heart" pattern, made by the Jefferson Glass Company of Toronto between 1913 and 1925. This pattern was originally produced in colourless or clear glass only and was unmarked.

The Royal Ontario Museum has reproduced a "Rayed Heart" pattern goblet, both in clear glass and in red, with a small ROM mark cast in relief on the base. The mark would not be difficult to grind off. On the top is an original Jefferson Glass Company goblet, with a red reproduction bottom left (a colour never originally produced), and a clear-glass reproduction bottom right. Reproduction pressed or mould-cast lamps and goblets are now produced by a number of companies, particularly in the United States.

Reproductions of intricate glass or ceramic patterns, made from copy moulds taken from original pieces, usually suffer some softening and loss of sharpness in the mould-making. Patterns of reproductions from new moulds usually differ in small details. Reproduction glass, as well, is usually chemically different from the originals. To a flicked fingernail, reproductions thus typically have a different ring from the originals, duller or sharper, and will usually also differ in weights and/or slightly in precise sizes. It is often necessary to compare them side by side or in photographs to spot these differences, however, so sharpness of pattern is the detail to be looked at first in initial examinations.

Just to illustrate the common differences found between genuine and reproduction glass and pottery, the following was noted when the clear-glass Jefferson "Rayed Heart" goblet was compared to the clear ROM reproduction.

	Height	Bowl diam.	Base diam.	Weight	Ring
Jefferson, original	146 mm	86 mm	78.5 mm	288 gm	dull
ROM reproduction	148 mm	84 mm	77.5 mm	340 gm	sharp

Royal Ontario Museum

the case of American patterns have now been examined and described according to direct comparison between reproductions and originals. That comparison is needed to determine differences such as sharpness of patterns, precise colours, exact dimensions, variations in ring tone, or relative weights. Still, great quantities of reproduction glass have long since entered the antiques market, where too often neither dealers nor collectors can be certain of what they have.

With the contemporary reproduction of simple everyday objects has come confusion in the antiques market. As mentioned earlier, many reproductions have been and are done as one-time productions by small companies or museums, often in limited quantities, and remain on the market only until supplies are exhausted. As a result, there is simply no way of keeping track of everything that has been or is being reproduced. Thus, any collector of anything has to be very careful in the mixture that is today's antiques market. Again, *caveat emptor*.

To summarize, as well as common acceptance and market-driven changes to the very definitions of the term "antique," there seem to be two sociological changes going on in the broader antiques market. First, a schism has occurred to the point that there are now two totally separate and distinct antiques markets. One is the market of Definition-1 antiques, based on age, quality, and rarity. This is the market of $3,000 to $5,000-and-up pieces of silver and furniture. Its players include the upper-level dealers, of whom there are probably fewer than a hundred in all of Canada, the upper-level and elitist collectors, including a few museums, and perhaps half a dozen major auction houses. This is the market of potential investment-quality antiques.

On the other side of the divide is the Definition-3 market, based primarily on object obsolescence rather than age and, to a high degree, geared to collecting fashion. This is the anything-goes market, which includes the great majority of dealers, certainly hundreds of auctioneers, and many tens of thousands of collectors of virtually everything ever produced.

Second, truly Definition-1 antiques and high-value pieces now seem almost a monopoly preserve of upper-level dealers, auction houses, and collectors. The far broader Definition-3 antiques market, however, with its thousands of dealers and shops, seems to be in a period of blending, with increasing true homogenization of antiques, reproductions, and whatever else may work in. When the attributes that matter to most antiques buyers and collectors are fashion, image, and decor-potential, age and originality become far less important. A good indication of this blending can be seen in the naming of some shops I have seen, such as "Antique Boutique," "Something Old – Something New," "Antiques and Reproductions," "Treasures & Collectibles," "Future Heirlooms," "Future Antiques," "Antiques 2000," "Antiques & Collectibles," or "Antiques Un-Ltd."

In particular, differences in age and construction of similar forms, original versus reproduction, mellow and blend with age and become less important with time. With increasing age, reproductions become ever less distinguishable from genuine antiques.

When reproductions will do as well as originals for the purposes of many buyers, the question then arises whether there is any point in differentiating between the two. Given approximately the same prices in the antiques market, does it really matter whether an oak roll-cover desk is late nineteenth century or a new reproduction (as long as the roll-cover is functional)? With factory-manufactured objects such as brass beds or pressed-back chairs, neither of which are the creations of individual craftsmen, will there be any substantial difference in fifty years between virtually identical objects based just on several decades difference in their ages? Both represent the same style and time period, consumer tastes, economy, and manufacturing technology. Thus, for reproductions of originally manufactured mass-market consumer goods, I have my doubts that the actual time of manufacturing will ultimately make much difference.

Reproductions of objects originally made during the pre-industrial craft period, by individual artisans and craftsmen, are a very different proposition. These reproductions are going to cause increasing problems of identification in the future, and already are. Does it matter whether a pine "harvest table" dates from the middle nineteenth century or is new but made of old wood? To a decor-oriented buyer, perhaps not. To an historian-antiquarian, however, the original table is a document that speaks of the age, culture, economy, and technology that produced it. The old-wood reproduction tells us nothing as a document, except that its copyist was a good craftsman. Reproductions that are identical in materials, design, construction and assembly techniques are the true FutureFakes, once they appear as early and genuine in the antiques market (as they already have). With increasing age they will become the most difficult of pieces to identify as genuine or fake. The present problems of identifying reproductions as fakes are nothing compared to what will face coming generations of antiquarians.

5

What to Look For:
Some Notes on Disaster Avoidance

———————

"He who would distinguish the true from the false must have an adequate idea of what is true and false."
— Benedict Spinoza (1632–1677) in *Ethics*, 1677

An Ontario collector recently bought a very fine, small curly-maple-and-mahogany side table at an auction. The table had delicately turned Sheraton legs that extended from all four corners, and all four sides were serpentine-bowed. The table was entirely of curly maple, except for mahogany-veneer banding around the drawer front and turned mahogany drawer knobs. Stylistically the piece dated from between 1810 and 1820. In the auction catalogue, it had been described as being from Eastern Ontario, and, if true, that would have made it one of the finest early Ontario small side tables ever to emerge.

Almost as soon as he got his expensive purchase home, the collector began to have doubts, not about whether the table was genuine, which it certainly was, but about its stated origin and whether it was actually Canadian. He called me, and brought along the table's single drawer. Drawers, and their woods and construction, are often the best focus points in examining furniture. The drawer turned out to be from the same table I had seen illustrated in the auction catalogue, and I had thought then it was perhaps American rather than from Eastern Ontario. I hadn't actually seen the piece or attended that auction, and I'd wondered who had acquired that table.

The drawer was very illustrative. First, the serpentine bowing of the front was a separate piece of wood, glued to a flat drawer front. Serpentine bowing is rare on Canadian furniture, and invariably is block-carved from a single piece of wood or formed from small sections glue-laminated together. Because of the impediment of the St. Lawrence Rapids, mahogany was also unavailable in Ontario before completion of the Lachine Canal at Montreal and the New York Erie Canal, both opened in 1825. Mahogany is rarely found in Ontario furniture much before about 1835 to 1840. Any darker wood found on an earlier Ontario Sheraton table I would expect to be native cherry or walnut, from trees that grow in Ontario.

The table's drawer bottom was pine, just as I would have expected, for pine was by far the most common secondary (hidden or structural) wood used in all early Canadian (and American) furniture. The drawer sides, front, and back, however, were of poplar, more common in northeastern American furniture. On the other hand, poplar is very uncommon in earlier Canadian furniture, particularly mixed with a pine drawer bottom, and I had never seen poplar in a Canadian piece as early in date as this table.

So, just as the collector had suspected, all of the little clues pointed to this being an American table. The general style and proportions of the table, the four serpentine sides, the extended Sheraton legs, the mix of maple and mahogany, and the two secondary woods all further pointed to it being a New England table, probably of Massachusetts or possibly New Hampshire origin.

In a case like this, with no attributed maker and no provenance, a full or absolutely proof-positive identification is impossible. When there is no inconsistency in the evidence the piece offers, however, and all of the clues pretty well point in the same direction, we come down instead to a "balance of probabilities" conclusion. That, rather than proof-positive or knowing absolutely, is usually the basis of attributions. The collector was delighted, of course, for from the auctioneer's mistake he had acquired a bargain, a quite genuine and fine table that in a New England auction sale would probably bring as much, in U.S. dollars, and possibly a good deal more than he had paid.

So, what do we look for in sorting out genuine pieces from fakes or partial fakery, or antique pieces from reproductions? There are all sorts of techniques of scientific analysis, often requiring sophisticated labs and equipment, but these are not usually available to the average antiques buyer or collector – except with considerable difficulty, time, and expense. Analytical techniques are also not usually available quickly, or *before* someone has decided and bought something, but only after the fact, when it is perhaps too late. Thus, what we have to look for in antiques examinations is entirely visual and tactile: what we can see and feel. Fortunately, good and thorough visual examination, and simple logical deduction, will usually sort out about 90 per cent of questions and problems.

The first requisite, and I can never reiterate this too strongly, is knowledge, from study, observation, and experience. Without knowing what you are looking for and at, you simply cannot spot fakery or close reproductions, any more than a mechanic can figure out what is wrong with your car or a surgeon can tell a diseased appendix from a normal one. Knowledge is requisite, though too many people fly blindly.

The first essential in considering any purchase, to my mind, is always to quiz the seller. Ask questions and cross-examine. Where did the seller/dealer get this piece? What does he/she know about its ownership history? Does the seller/dealer know what might have been done to it in the way of repair or restoration? Look for reactions as well as just answers. If the seller/dealer appears evasive, or perhaps suspiciously uncertain, or gets touchy about being questioned, it is probably time to move on.

Questioning, of course, is more difficult with auction houses, for the auctioneers are simply sales agents. Some auction houses have their own in-house experts or contract consultants. They are still prone to mistakes, however, because they rely heavily on descriptions, provenances, and attributions provided by consignor-sellers, who quite naturally try to shine the best light on the objects they are selling. Thus, even reading beyond the adjectives, buyers cannot rely on auction catalogue descriptions as absolute gospel, and mistakes are fairly common. That is how the collector of the Massachusetts maple side table lucked out, or how faked pieces (Figs. 6, 7, 10, 11, 14, 15, 17, 18) can and do pass undetected through otherwise perfectly honest auctions. The unreliability of catalogue descriptions is also a warning for buyers leaving absentee, or "order," bids for pieces they have never physically seen. Never, ever bid on a piece at auction that you have not examined.

Once questioning is exhausted, it comes time to examine any piece on its own merits. A small tool pouch is handy here (Fig. 38), which should include at least a tape measure, a pocketknife, a five-power or stronger magnifying glass, a pen-light flashlight, and a set of inside and outside callipers, as well as a vernier calliper.

Furniture

Since furniture is composed of many parts, it is both the most difficult to examine and the most difficult to be sure of. Furniture examination is made doubly difficult by the fact that virtually all craft-period furniture has been repaired at some point, and the older the furniture is, the more likely it is to have been repaired. Drawer runners, the wearing surfaces, have commonly been built up or replaced. Chair stretchers got broken, veneer segments came unglued and got lost, hardware came unscrewed and got misplaced, and nailed-on mouldings came loose and fell off. Few early couches or chairs exist that still have their original upholstery, or nineteenth-century chairs still with their original cane, splint, or rush seats.

Thus, early repairs should be expected in furniture, to the point that an absence of repairs in what appear to be very early pieces is itself grounds for suspicion. Early repairs, except that they may reduce condition and therefore value, are not fakery and do not mean that a piece has been altered or "upgraded." However, one problem in examining furniture is sorting out old repairs from more recent alteration or upgrading.

In examining furniture, *always* look at decorative elements first and ask yourself questions. Is any carving intaglio (cut into the surface) or in relief, above the surface? Intaglio carving is usually added fakery (Figs. 10, 17, 18). Does the carving match or does it appear cruder

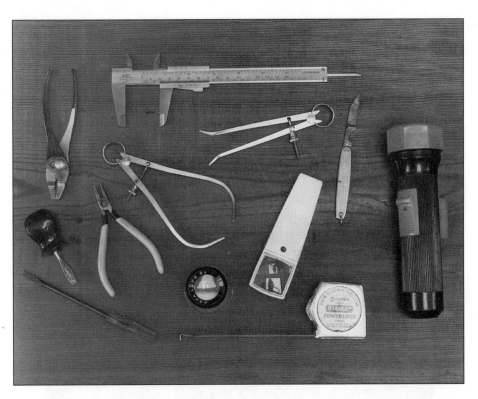

Fig. 38: Handy tools for examining antiques. At the top and centre are vernier, inside, and outside callipers, for gauging thicknesses and diameters. The pocket-knife is necessary for any poking, shaving, or scraping. Magnifiers are essential, including a battery-powered illuminated glass, for looking at everything from wood grain to prints and at markings and engraving. A combination imperial and metric tape measure is necessary. A flashlight, with good strong batteries, is essential for looking at interior areas and into hidden corners of furniture. The small screwdrivers and pliers are perhaps non-essentials, but one never knows, and it is often helpful to have them along. *Author's tool pouch*

Fig. 39: Most early furniture has been repaired at some point, and the older the furniture, the more likely are multiple repairs. This small mahogany-veneered American box desk of the 1790s shows several veneer repairs and replacements done at different times, and has been restored more than once. Mismatched or unblended repairs such as this will reduce the condition and therefore the value of an antique, but are still perfectly honest early repairs and do not indicate any form of upgrading fakery. *Author's collection*

(Figs. 10, 17) than the shaping and construction of the piece itself? If the skill level differs, the carving is probably added. Are veneers and inlays consistent in thickness and colour, or do some appear to be repair replacements or even later additions?

Do the back sides of drawer fronts show extra holes or earlier holes that have been plugged, indicating that knobs or hardware have been changed or improved or upgraded? Does the present brass, glass, or wooden-knob hardware have modern machine-threaded stems and nuts, indicating reproduction hardware? Before the factory-made furniture of the 1860s and later, the majority of Canadian furniture with drawers was equipped with turned wooden knobs, not more expensive brass hardware. Changing those original wooden knobs to more elaborate hardware is a favourite and very common dealer-improvement practice. If *all* hardware – knobs or pulls, hinges, locks, and castors – appears totally changed, then the piece is doubly suspicious, and there may be upgradings of actual structure (Fig. 6) as well.

Always look at the backs and undersides of furniture and any drawers, and at any and all hidden areas, with a flashlight. All craft-period or cabinetmaker-made furniture shows economy of labour. Makers simply did not lavish time on areas that did not show. Thus, the backboard outsides of cupboards, cabinets, and chests of drawers and the undersides of drawer bottoms are usually made of random-width and rough-sawed boards, neither planed nor sanded.

On Canadian furniture, this secondary, or non-visible, wood is pine, with only very rare exceptions until the industrial period. Mixed secondary woods, as in the pine-plus-poplar drawer of the New England table described earlier, are rare in Canadian furniture, though common in British or American pieces. The smoothing or finishing of non-visible areas came only with factories and powered equipment in the later nineteenth century. Thus, regardless of apparent style or period, furniture with planed or smoothed wood for backboard outer sides or drawer undersides is usually reproduction, however antique it may appear – or have become through age alone.

The wooden components of antique furniture usually run with the wood grain in directions of greatest strength. In a piece that is higher than it is wide, such as a tall cupboard or an armoire, backboards typically run horizontally, across the shortest span. With a piece or section wider than it is high, such as a chest of drawers, backboards and wood grain usually run vertically. The grain of drawer structures is always horizontal, while that of panels is always vertical. Thus, if you see a piece with rectangular cupboard door panels but with the panel grain running horizontally (Fig. 15), you can immediately conclude that the panels are replacements and wrongly done.

The species of woods used in combination is important. Woods used in craft-period furniture, and before the coming of railroads, did not travel very far, except as logs going to sawmills, downstream on creeks and rivers. The overland roads and trails of the nineteenth century were mud, snow, dust, or ruts, in season. Roads were just not suitable for transporting heavy cargoes, so that all movement of logs or lumber was by water.

Native woods are few enough that most can be identified visually, most of the time. Unfinished rather than finished surfaces are also best for visual identifications. There was no early importation of exotic woods, except mahogany into the Maritimes and as far west as the seagoing port of Montreal. Beyond that were the Lachine Rapids. Thus, anywhere away from the immediate areas of seaports, Canadian furniture was dependent on native woods. Given that logs and lumber were not transported great distances, or at all except by water, those native woods were also from tree species that *all* grew within the same natural geographic range.

A reasonable ability to identify woods is essential for anyone collecting or dealing with furniture. Though not all woods are always identifiable by eye alone, with increasing experience many can be. Therefore, everyone concerned with furniture should have one or a few books on native trees, such as those listed in the bibliography. A wood identification kit, comprised of small, smooth but unfinished two-by-three-inch (5-by-7.5-cm) wood samples, is even more essential for making comparisons. Kits, including over thirty samples, are available at reasonable cost from the Eastern Forest Products Laboratory in Ottawa.

In looking at the unfinished wood surfaces in furniture (with secondary pine as a universal wood), I could be comfortable seeing mixed maple, birch, cherry, or walnut in the same Ontario piece. Maple, birch, butternut, or rarely cherry would make sense in a Quebec piece, and maple, birch, or imported mahogany could all be expected in a Nova Scotia piece. The use, however, of any wood that is *not* native to the area the furniture is purportedly from, or that cannot be explained, raises an immediate question: *How* did that wood get into this piece of furniture? Thus, I would not expect to see walnut in a Quebec piece, or butternut in Nova Scotia furniture, because those areas are outside the natural ranges of those trees.

That *how* was the first question raised by our collector's auction bargain. How did mahogany and poplar get into an 1810-to-1820 period table, supposedly from Ontario, when mahogany was unavailable in Ontario at that time, and poplar was not used? It became an unanswerable question, and thus a clue pointing in a different direction.

Since pine is the most common wood of Canadian furniture, I outlined, in Chapter 3, English and European furniture made of Scots pine, much of which has come into the North American antiques market. Where the North American and European styles are very similar, as with simple wall or corner cupboards or basic pine tables or stools, it is impossible to positively distinguish the differences stylistically. The grain appearance of European Scots pine and Canadian White pine are also too similar for reliable visual judgements. This is where wood-cell analysis comes in. Just as the needles, cones, twigs, or bark of all pines are different, so are the individual cells of the wood, as they appear when examined and identified under a microscope. Wood-cell analysis is the only reliable method of determining absolutely the species of various pines, or of any woods.

Wood-cell analysis, though a visual identification, requires a laboratory and a knowledge of the cell structure of wood. An analyst first puts a small sliver, taken from a piece of furniture, into a vial of acetic acid. In a couple of days the sliver will break down into what appears as a blob of mush, really the individual cells of the wood. With tweezers, the analyst will then put a bit of the mush on a glass microscope slide, spread it thinly, and stain it with a drop of orange stain for contrast. Looked at through a thirty- to fifty-power microscope, the individual cells can then be compared and identified, usually to the genus, and often to the exact species, of the tree the sliver came from.

Wood-cell analysis is a very useful technique for identifying woods that cannot be absolutely determined visually – like the various pines. For the average collector, however, it is not practical, since the analysis requires time, finding a laboratory and analyst, and some cost.

A piece of furniture made of Scots pine is certainly of English or European origin, since the species was not introduced into North America until the late nineteenth century. The opposite, however, is not true. If you identify the wood as North American White pine, it does not necessarily mean the piece is American or Canadian. During the late eighteenth and first half of the nineteenth century, huge quanties of North American lumber, primarily pine, were shipped to England and Europe, mostly for house- and shipbuilding. Some, however, wound up being made into furniture, English furniture of North American pine.

In the nineteenth century, during the age of massive cutting of old-growth forests to create new agricultural land, completely clear and knot-free lumber, in very wide boards, was readily available. Because there was no need, cabinetmakers simply *did not use* lumber or boards with knots, particularly in areas of furniture that showed. Knots are ugly intrusions in the otherwise smooth surfaces of furniture, and larger knots dry and fall out, leaving holes. With pine, a maker might occasionally have used boards with one or two very small and stable knots for hidden backboards or drawer bottoms, but otherwise never, not even in the roughest country furniture. There was no wood scarcity and therefore no need to use wood with knots. Thus, knots in Canadian furniture, though not necessarily a sign of fakery, are usually a sign of replacement, repair, or poor restoration, using either low quality or modern woods.

When you look at any piece of furniture, and particularly one that has the potential of having been upgraded, married, divorced, or made up, unfinished areas usually hold the clues. The colours, or colour differences or contrasts, of never-finished wood in non-visible areas are one vital indicator. The age patina created by air, light, and fireplace or woodstove smoke exposure over many decades always discoloured and darkened wood surfaces, and that discolouration is virtually impossible to duplicate or fake (though LaMontagne managed it with his "Great Brewster Chair"). If, in surveying the backs, insides, and undersides of furniture, you find that the colours of the wood do not reasonably match or blend, then it becomes pretty obvious that something is wrong, and that some wood is newer or from a different source than the other.

The secretary-desk in Figures 14 and 14a is a good example. The unfinished backboards of both the upper and lower sections are old and genuine, and appear original to those sections. As well as the saw cuttings being different, however, the patina colour of the backboards of the upper section is considerably lighter than that of the boards in the lower section. This is a sure indication that the two sections have not always been together. Instead, they came from two different pieces and places and have more recently been married. The unfinished back edge of the desk top, though of cherry, a relatively dark wood, is still lighter in colour than the pine backboards of either section. With no age patina whatever, the desk top is clearly quite new and of new wood.

Another good indication of either early repairs or, more often, marriage is extra and unused screw holes – not those in drawer fronts, indicating changed hardware, but any others. Most particularly, the tops of tables of all types, and of chests of drawers and sideboards, were typically attached by screws running from the inside of the frame at an upward and outward angle into the underside of the table, chest, or sideboard tops.

Before the 1860s, screws were blunt-tipped and often hand-threaded, usable only in pre-drilled holes. Pointed and self-tapping screws are post-1860s. Screws, however, can be replaced and often were, and new screws can be ground down to blunt the tips. Nails, likewise though not extensively used in furniture, are also roughly datable, but also replaceable. Dealers often tout the virtues of blacksmith-made, or "rose-headed," nails as evidence of age, though handmade nails are often salvaged from old buildings and barns. The sharp-eyed can even find them lying on the ground at many eighteenth-century historical sites. Handmade screws and nails, if genuine, can be dating evidence for furniture, but they are hardly conclusive. Old screws or nails can easily be added in upgrading fakery. As well, the presence of modern screws or nails does not necessarily mean fakery and more often indicates earlier repairs rather than the fact that a piece has been altered or faked.

Screws and nails, overall, are less important than extra but unexplained holes. If a table, chest of drawers, or sideboard top, after it is unscrewed (whatever the actual screws) from the frame or base, shows *extra* screw holes, more screw holes and in different positions than those matching in the frame for the current top attachment, then they raise immediate questions. Why are those extra holes there? What were they for? The extra holes usually indicate that the top, though perhaps old itself, had once been attached to a different frame. The conclusion is that this has to be a different top, now attached and married to the current frame. Early replacements of furniture tops or more recent marriages are quite common, for tops often split or warped, or screws loosened and fell out, allowing tops to get separated from their original bases or frames.

The basic rule is that *any* extra or older holes in furniture, wherever they are, need to be explained. That applies not just to screw holes, but also to cuts for previous hinges or locks or even to strange nails or old nail holes (not common in any but homemade furniture or repairs). The questions raised by unexplained holes have to be reasonably resolved, perhaps by identifying early repairs, or parts or hardware now missing. Unresolved, these questions leave an underlying suspicion that a piece has been altered or is married, divorced, or perhaps made up from several pieces of furniture.

Dating of furniture is rarely absolute. Date spreads of ten or fifteen years are about the narrowest one can determine, and often, with country furniture of long-lived traditional designs, spreads of even fifty years are the closest anyone can arrive at.

Construction of furniture – from the centuries-old methods of hand-cut mortise-and-tenon and dovetailed joints of pre-industrial craft-period furniture to the dowelled joints (Figs. 40, 41) and machine-cut dovetailing (Fig. 43) of later-nineteenth-century manufactured furniture and reproductions – changed because of mechanization, but only gradually. Some writers try to date nineteenth- and early-twentieth-century furniture by nails, screws, hinges, and joint types. That, however, is too simplistic. For one thing, many elements of furniture could be and were changed as part of early repairs, including replacement of drawer pulls and runners.

Changes in furniture-making technology, mechanization, and construction also came much more slowly and gradually than changes in furniture styles and fashions. Styles and designs are more accurately datable. Because of this, furniture of the second half of the nineteenth century often shows mixed or transitional joints and construction methods, both old and new techniques combined in the same piece.

I have an American mahogany Hepplewhite sideboard that my mother bought as a quite genuine Federal-period piece of 1800 to 1810, for $75 in Boston in 1928. She never really examined her treasured sideboard, nor did I, until after I inherited and started restoring it. When I was examining and reglueing loose joints, I found that the sideboard had both traditional mortise-and-tenon joints, as well as some more modern dowelled joints (Fig. 40). Dowelled joints, with short dowels glued into opposing holes in two pieces to be joined, are simpler to manufacture, and are an element of mass-production that was introduced only in the 1870s. Dowelled joints in pieces of much earlier styles are a sure sign of reproductions, and are still a standard method of joining in manufactured furniture (Fig. 41).

My mother's sideboard has also had every piece of wood in it, including backboards, smoothed by both hand and powered planing, and the insides of both the cabinet and drawers were also originally varnished. The veneers vary in thickness, with both thin roll-cut and thicker sawed types. Both hinges and locks are clearly original to the piece, and are attached with their small 1870s or 1880s pointed self-tapping screws. The pressed-brass drawer pulls, also original to the sideboard, have machine-threaded posts but hand-filed retaining nuts.

Fig. 40: Changes in furniture materials and construction came with the appearance of new forms of powered machinery and the adoption of mass-production techniques. One such change was the replacement of cabinetmakers' mortise-and-tenon joints with glued dowel joints. This illustration is of the back of my "Centennial" reproduction sideboard of the 1870s (Chapter 5). Old glue has loosened, allowing a back corner leg to separate from the frame. The two dowels connecting leg and frame became visible, a certain indication that the sideboard is a nineteenth-century reproduction.

Construction techniques must be viewed with caution, for the appearance of new machinery did not bring changes in construction methods either swiftly or universally. There were long transition periods, and, in furniture made from the 1860s to the 1930s, both older craft-period and newer mechanized construction details can often be found in the same piece of furniture. Thus, construction details are good only as relative, but not absolute, dating evidence. Generally speaking, and excepting later repairs, it is the latest characteristic that governs the date of any piece of furniture. With this sideboard, the 1800-period Hepplewhite style must be discounted for dating when the dowelled construction and machine-planed backboards indicate the piece could not be earlier than the 1870s. *Author's collection*

Fig. 41: Most factory-made or manufactured furniture, since about the 1870s, has been assembled with glued dowels rather than hand-cut mortise-and-tenon joints. The dowels, in this illustration, are inserted into the top of an unfinished cabriole leg for a reproduction chair. The exposed dowel ends will later be glued into seat-frame segments.

The modern dowelled joint is weaker than earlier mortise-and-tenon joints. Particularly when combined with dried-out, older animal-based glues, dowelled joints often become loose or the dowels break off. A glimpse of a dowel in the thin crack opened by a loose joint is a give-away that a supposedly antique piece is a reproduction. *Author's files*

Fig. 42: Dovetailing was the standard method of joining drawer segments, and often other furniture parts. Dovetailing generally became smaller and finer from the seventeenth through the twentieth centuries. Dovetails of the seventeenth century are generally single, wide, and often roughly cut. By the mid-eighteenth century, dovetails had become smaller, and multiple, usually two to four for each joint. This drawer side shows the hand-cut dovetailing of a 1770s maple slant-front desk, with a scored mark as a guide to dovetailing depth. The wearing surface of the drawer bottom has been spliced and repaired, a repair that was virtually universal on early drawers. *Author's collection*

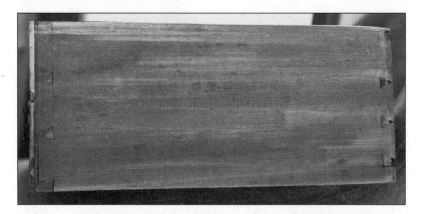

Fig. 43: It is typically believed that earlier hand-cut dovetailing shows scoring marks as a guide to the cabinetmaker, while later machine-cut dovetailing does not. Like many other construction details, however, there were no absolutes, and many types of twentieth-century woodworking machines were and are hand-guided. Thus, except in the use of largely automated machinery, various cabinetmakers' marks were and are still necessary. The dovetailing depth marks on this drawer from a 1930s reproduction Chippendale desk are no different than those of two centuries earlier, though the absolute sameness of the dovetails indicates that they were machine-cut. *Private collection*

Fig. 44: The back side of a drawer, from a late-seventeenth-century American oak chest of drawers, shows the straight saw-blade marks of a two-man pit saw or a frame saw. Pit or frame saws, used entirely by hand, prevailed in Canada until water-powered single-bladed or gang saws appeared in the early nineteenth century. Even then, hand-operated saws for cutting lumber remained in use until around 1900, long after the appearance of water- or steam-powered saws. *Author's collection*

Fig. 45: The saw marks of this pine drawer bottom, long and straight, indicate lumber cut with a straight-bladed saw, probably a water- or steam-powered reciprocating gang saw. The sawing is from the late 1870s or early 1880s. The drawer, also with hand-cut dovetailing, is from my mother's "Centennial" reproduction Hepplewhite sideboard (Chapter 5). The same piece has modern dowelled leg-and-case joining (Fig. 40). *Author's collection*

Thus, everything about my mother's sideboard, though it is an elegant piece and stylistically quite accurate, indicates it is an American "Centennial" reproduction of the late 1870s or 1880s, exactly the period of transition in cabinetmaking technology and machinery. One of the biggest dealers in 1920s Boston had sold my mother a fifty-year-old reproduction, with the assurance of it being a genuine 1800-to-1810 Hepplewhite piece – and at the price (then) of a genuine piece. By definition, it became a fake, just from the deceptive way it was sold. Now that I know it is a reproduction, it is no longer a fake. My mother also remained satisfied throughout her life that her sideboard was genuine, so I guess no harm was done.

The transitional technology and construction methods evident in the sideboard point up the mistake that is often made in using the mechanization of cabinetmaking as conclusive evidence for dating furniture. We cannot link the known dates of invention and first introduction of new machinery too closely to the actual time frames of that machinery's widespread acceptance and use. The two often differed by as much as a century. Largely for reasons of cost and production-scale, new technology and mechanization came very slowly to furniture-making, an industry with many small-scale producers, which to this day is still very labour-intensive.

A brief diversion into backgrounds seems appropriate here. Modern technological innovations, such as television, hand-held calculators, microwave ovens, or computers, can achieve rapid acceptance once they are introduced, largely because we have long since had, accepted, and standardized their basic power source: electricity. The nineteenth century, however, as well as being an age of transition from craft to factory, and from hand tools to powered machinery, also experienced several transitions in basic power sources. The century progressed from human, animal, and water power, then to steam engines, and finally to electric motors and internal-combustion engines – the latter only during the last twenty years of the century.

Steam was expensive, both in the capital cost of engines and boilers and of fuel, while water power was cheap or free. New machines were expensive, but undeveloped. The first continuous-cutting rotary saw, for example, appeared in the 1790s and the bandsaw in 1808, but neither became fully practical until the development of high-speed power sources and improved metallurgy. Advances in metallurgy caught up fifty years later, with the development of flexible (not easily breakable) but hard steel (which retained sharpness) for saw blades.

Steam engines provided (for the period) limitless power, but factory power-transmission systems, from engines to machinery, were great complexes of drive shafts, pulleys, and belts. Because of weight and friction, these systems were massively inefficient. A steam-powered system could run dozens or perhaps hundreds of machines, but all the shafts and pulleys had to be kept fully running, even if only one machine was actually in use. Like water-powered saw or grist mills, just driving factory power-transmission systems could often require up to 75 per cent of the actual power produced at source, before it ever got to the machines. Friction absorbed the rest. Thus, steam, like water power, had very low efficiency from source power to delivered and usable power.

Little wonder that small industries or workshops, including small-scale operations such as cabinetmaking, neither saw the need in an age of cheap labour nor could afford the upfront costs of equipping them-selves with expensive steam engines, power-transmission systems, or high-capacity new machinery. Many small woodworking-shop machines were invented and predated the electric motor by a century or more, but most were individually powered by hands or feet, with simple pulleys and belts, treadles, or bicycle-like pedalled cranks.

It was the electric motor after the 1880s and 1890s, providing each machine with its own independent and inexpensive power source with nothing but a cord and switch, that really made mechanization of the cabinetmaking industry cost-effective. Even then, electrifi-cation took forty to fifty years to largely replace earlier water- or steam-powered systems and machinery. The same cost-benefit con-siderations are current today, for example, in the high upfront capital costs of computerized robot-equipped factory assembly lines versus the ongoing costs of labour-intensive assembly lines in low-wage countries.

Back to furniture. Sawing and smoothing is often a clue to originality, replacement, reproduction, or fakery. Saw marks on unfinished sections such as backboards may be straight but irregular and unevenly spaced. That indicates handsawing, whether by a pit saw cutting lumber or a frame saw or carpenter's saw in a cabinet shop (Fig. 44). Saw marks may also be straight but evenly spaced and regular, indicating the lumber was cut with a water-powered reciprocating single-bladed or gang saw (Figs. 14a, 45), and that it probably predates 1900. Slightly curved marks indicate cutting with a circular or rotary saw, with the cutting probably postdating the 1870s or 1880s (Fig. 14a).

Furniture datings from saw marks cannot be precise, however, but only relative, one type to another. Lumber cutting went through over a century of transition, from hand-cutting to water-powered gang saws to steam- or electric-powered circular or band saws. All three methods, still including even ancient and laborious pit-sawing, were also in simultaneous use through the later nineteenth century.

Early lumber, cut either by hand or with somewhat primitive machinery, typically also varied slightly in thickness and width, which can often still be seen in the finished furniture. A simple calliper will indicate expected variations in the thickness of, say, the planks of an early pine tabletop, as opposed to the very precise thickness and width of more modern lumber.

Wood also shrinks with age, always laterally, across the grain. This is noticeable with such parts as cupboard panels, which become loose in their frames, or backboards that shrink cross-grain to leave open gaps. Lateral shrinkage also occurs with round lathe turnings, which will gradually flatten slightly to assume an ovoid, or egg-shaped, cross-section. Callipers are essential to detect this. An old round turning will have a slightly smaller diameter gauged across one quadrant than across the other, while the turning of a leg or stretcher of a recent reproduction (Figs. 27, 33) will still largely be round. The shrinkage usually takes several decades, and differences of cross-section diameters are very useful in determining whether a turning is old and presumably original or a replacement or part of a reproduction.

Sanding of surfaces that were to be finished on finer craft-period work was done with damp sand or sandstone, which was rubbed around, using ever-finer grits down to pumice dust. Non-visible surfaces, however, if they were to be smoothed rather than left rough-sawed, were usually only surface planed with a wide-bladed block plane. Most pine furniture, destined for painting, was often finish-planed overall, but not finally sanded. Though a good planer could achieve very flat and smooth surfaces, the planing marks are still usually visible in very oblique light or can be felt with one's fingertips. Planing was very laborious, which is why non-visible parts of early furniture, such as drawer bottoms or cupboard backboards, were left rough-sawed.

On the other hand, if most or all parts, even hidden parts, are smoothed, sanded, or perhaps even painted or varnished, that is a definite clue to either modern (since the 1870s) factory manufacturing or, if the style is much earlier, to a late-nineteenth-century or more recent reproduction.

Paints or dark finishes are insidious, for they can cover a plethora of sins. Reproduction "original" paints in old reds, blues, or greens are not hard to mix from pigments and to apply with rags. Old milk-based paints, with organic or metallic-oxide colours, are now even available commercially, in cans. Thus, reproduced painting, with the logical wear spots artificially worn, can easily cover new work, particularly on pine furniture (Fig. 18). Reproducing dark Victorian varnishes, usually with a stain mixed right into the varnish, is equally easy. So, with paints or dark varnishes, another standard rule is always to look beyond them to the unfinished surfaces.

A couple once called me about a Quebec diamond-point-panelled armoire they had found with a dealer. They had somehow cajoled the dealer into letting them take away a door for a week on approval, with a 20-per-cent down payment, and were thinking seriously of buying the piece. I liked the tactic, for while the couple had a week to seek other opinions and decide, without a door the dealer could not sell the armoire out from under them.

As with any diamond-point-panelled piece in the current market, the armoire was very expensive, and anything expensive should be questioned. The couple was not suspicious, but sensibly just careful. I asked them to bring along the door and some photographs of the whole piece, which they did.

The armoire, from the better-than-usual photographs, looked good. It was, however, painted with a very dark-green "original" paint that lacked wear spots where one would normally expect them. The paint colour was wrong as well, much too dark and opaque for early copper-oxide green colouring. From the probable early-eighteenth-century date of the armoire, the paint was also just too unworn and unbattered and – for "original" paint – far too clean and perfect to reflect two and a half centuries of use, greasy hands, and household grunge.

The side panels of the armoire were plain and rectangular, which was typical of such pieces and certainly genuine. Given the lighting of the photographs, I could see old scrapes and nicks, but evidently *under*, not over or through, the covering paint. The armoire had clearly been repainted, though the couple said the dealer professed the paint to be original.

Since they were the prime decorative element that made the armoire expensive, however, the diamond-point panels of the doors were what warranted the closest look. The panels were good, well cut, sanded, and smooth, but without any of the nicks and scars under the paint that I had noticed in the photographs of the side panels. Strange. Why? The insides or backsides of the door frames and panels were unpainted. That was fine, for armoire insides and door backsides were rarely originally painted. The backs of the door panels were both edge-bevelled, and showed hand-planing marks, just as one would expect. In the bright sunlight, though, sitting in the rear of the couple's station wagon, the door backs showed three odd anomalies.

All armoires, in fact most early furniture from any western culture, were constructed with mortise-and-tenon joints, which were then drilled through and pinned together tightly with wooden pins cut off flush with the wood surfaces. The pins were typically hand-whittled and were never perfectly round or straight. The pins of the armoire door, however, were perfectly round and their ends recently cut. They were short pieces of modern dowels (Fig. 10), cut flush, and overpainted on the door front. Obviously someone had knocked out the original pins, disassembled the door frame, and then reassembled it with new pieces of dowel as replacement pins. Why disassemble the door frame, except to remove the original panels?

Second, the backs of the panels, but not the door frames, seemed to have been lightly stained with some weak solution, maybe tea or coffee. The staining appeared to be perhaps an attempt to add some age patina to freshly surface-planed wood. It did not work very well, for it still looked like tea or coffee staining. The staining also meant that the panel-backs were now slightly darker in colour than the wood of the door frames. That contrast raised the immediate supposition that these panels had not always been in these door frames.

The panels, as is often the case, were slightly loose in the slots of their framing. When I worked a panel a bit to one side in its slot, I could see that the panel staining ran edge to edge; it extended beyond the visible part of the panel backs and right into the tight frame slots. Real age patina would typically have been much lighter in the hidden frame slots. The panel backs had obviously been stained while they were out of the door frames or before they went in.

When we are looking at antiques with an eye to whether they are fakes or reproductions, as outlined earlier, we cannot always come down to proof-positive conclusions. We are dealing, instead, with various bits of evidence, sometimes inconclusive or even contradictory, and from that evidence we must try to put together a balance of probabilities. There were any number of possible reasons why this armoire door had been disassembled and then reassembled with modern dowels for pins. Maybe the door had to be taken apart for cleaning. Maybe the original pins got mixed up, lost, or were too shrunken with age to reinsert. Maybe the original paint was too worn and scruffy for the armoire to be saleable, so it had to be either stripped or given a fresh painting.

Still, the unanswered questions remained. Why did the flat side panels have old nicks and scrapes under the paint, but the diamond-point door panels were smooth and pristine? Since they purported to be original, why were the door-panel backs stained at all, and obviously while the panels were out of the door frame? Why was there a need for the apparent attempt to blend together age-patina colours between the panel backs and door frames?

No matter how we looked at the armoire door, and considered options, the strong *balance of probabilities* that emerged here was that the diamond-point door panels, but only the panels, were recently made fakes. The painting and staining was cover-up. The original rectangular flat door panels, which probably matched the side panels, had been removed, and the new diamond-point panels added, increasing the value of the otherwise genuine armoire by ten times that of a plain flat-panelled piece.

From a follow-up report, I learned later that the dealer who owned the armoire was incredulous and unbelieving; perhaps it was just an act, or perhaps he really didn't know. In any event, the couple returned the door and got back their down payment. Where the armoire may be now, I don't know.

Silver and Metals

Silver is relatively easier to examine than furniture, simply because there are fewer focus points to look at. First, the total faking of silver is extremely difficult to accomplish and carry off successfully. Unlike Canadian furniture, where moderately priced pine "harvest" tables are probably the most often faked for a high-volume market, faking or fakery of Canadian (or any) silver, because of the difficulty, is usually limited to the pieces that have the highest potential value. At this level, collectors are also typically quite expert in their specialties, and interested buyers are most likely to examine possible purchases very carefully.

The four prime focal points in looking at silver are: style, colour differences, marks, and usage and wear. Taken together, this presents some difficulty for the silver faker. It means, first, that he has to come up with exactly the right period and style of piece – itself probably antique – to fake. There would be no point in applying an eighteenth-century maker's punch-mark on a piece of silver that, stylistically, was from the mid- or late-nineteenth century. That would make about as much sense as applying a counterfeit Thomas Nisbet label to a plain pine table, something Nisbet never made.

Styles in silver changed fairly rapidly from the seventeenth to nine-teenth century, as did silversmithing technology and methods. Most silversmiths' working dates are now known and published. Thus, age gaps between known maker dates and the time periods of silver styles would be immediately apparent to anyone who knew antique silver. The style-date versus mark-date was the first give-away with the Schindler plate in Chapter 3.

Repairs or alterations, too, very typically show visually. Most honest repairs involve resoldering of feet, handles, spouts, or lid finials or reattaching of appliqués. The silver solder used is typically modern sterling (.925 pure) or coin silver (.975 pure), while early silver, as noted earlier, often had a lower silver content and unknown impurities. Soldered repairs or alterations typically show thin soldered seams, or filled spots or sections, that are often slightly different in colour from the original silver. Because of that, any colour variations or discoloured sections in antique silver should always raise the questions of what was done, and why.

An exception to this is Indian trade silver, of which many or most pieces have been buried for many years and then excavated. Silver first tarnishes nearly to black and, buried or lost in moist conditions, devel-ops corrosion pitting. Most genuine trade silver, no matter how recently polished, is going to show some corrosion pitting and flaking from long exposure to weather or burial. In examining trade silver and its condition, remember the old adage: "If it looks too good to be true, it probably is."

Marks are also a difficult proposition for the faker. Most fake marks are punched with new and reasonably sharp steel punch-stamps. Few original makers' punches survive, and most of those are well worn – and in museum collections. New silver-mark punches, like all "exact" reproductions, usually vary slightly from the originals in shape, size, or letter placement (Fig. 46a). Doubtful punch-marks can be compared with photographs of original marks in John Langdon's *Canadian Silversmiths, 1700–1900* and other books.

Most early silver, particularly that of Britain, Europe, and North America, was originally maker-stamped, sometimes using as many as six different punches, including date-code letters on British silver. Thus, the faker, possessing an original piece that, just to add value, could perhaps bear faking with different makers' marks, faces two judgement calls. First, is the piece with new fake marks going to be substantially more valuable than the otherwise genuine piece with its original marks? Will that potential value difference then justify the trouble and effort of the faking? If the answer seems yes, then comes the problem of how to get rid of the original marks.

As outlined in Chapter 3, original marks that are erased in favour of fake marks are usually removed by one of three methods: either grinding away and polishing over, filling in old marks with new silver, or, less commonly, lifting and inserting genuine marks from some piece of much lower value. Grinding out old marks leaves slight depressions in the surface of the silver, which are visible in very oblique light or are detectable by feel. Filling in, unless the infilling is composed of substantially the same content of silver and trace impurities as the silver to be filled, can leave visible discolourations, brighter or darker than the piece of silver itself. Lifting and inserting marks can leave seams or pockets around the marks as evidence of recent soldering.

Most early Canadian silver – particularly larger pieces – is light and quite thin, showing the economy of material used by a craft that depended on melting down miscellaneous old coinage and scrap silver as the only source of raw material. Maker punch-marking in thin soft silver was usually done quite gently, and the markings were typically shallow. Neither makers nor customers wanted punches so heavy and deep that they showed through to the side opposite the mark. Punch-marking, as well, was often done quickly and not quite squarely, so that marks are typically deeper on one side than the other.

Add to shallow original punch-marks a century or two of necessary polishing, often with abrasive cleaners, and everything grows blurry. Makers' marks, like any engraving, become gradually softer and less distinct with repeated polishing, sometimes even to the point at which they are difficult to distinguish or identify (as the worn coins, Fig. 3).

Thus, crisp or nicely distinct marks on otherwise-much-polished or worn silver (or other metals) are a solid clue that the marks, or perhaps the engraving, may be a lot newer than the silver itself. A first question for anyone looking at a piece of early silver is: What makes the value of the piece? Is it rarity of the object itself or its maker's mark or engraving? If the value comes down mainly to the mark or engraving, then the piece should be doubly and triply examined.

Recently I had a chance to look at a large silver plate (Fig. 46) that was a master work, for it combined just about every element seen in fake silver, all of it quite obvious. With a scalloped rim, the plate had a single crisp mark of Jean François Landron (1686–1761). Landron was a Quebec City silversmith of the New France period, and only about a dozen of his pieces are known today.

Viewed from the back, the silver of the whole outer half of the scalloped rim was a different colour than the inner rim and the bowl, indicating that the entire rim had been massively repaired or that the faker had created an entirely new rim. Perhaps the original rim was too plain and round, though that would have been much more accurate for the New France period. There was no way to tell. The scalloped rim now on the plate, however, was a style that first appeared in the 1760s and 1770s, on English ceramics, well after Landron was dead. The rim was also not consistently shaped or finished.

The mark was a beauty, squarely, evenly, and quite deeply punched, and was nice and distinct, easily readable even without a magnifier (Fig. 46a). The plate itself, for that matter, was quite clean of wear or abrasion and hardly showed the mellowing one would expect from two and a half centuries of use and polishing.

The plate had also been getting around. After I had looked at it, I discovered that a colleague in another museum, who was far more of a silver specialist than I, had also examined it a few months earlier. He had also felt that the mark was a fake, on a plate with a severely rebuilt or altered rim. He thought, too, that the plate was probably earlier twentieth century, not really antique, and of South American origin. Rather than being a falsely marked but otherwise genuine piece, this plate was a total fake – plate, rim, and mark together.

With silver, or any other metals, anything that appears as funny or wrong should raise questions. Unlike the very widespread alteration or upgrading of furniture, faking of Canadian silver, beyond simple and obvious repairs, is not as common. As mentioned earlier, table flatware and small pieces are generally safe from faking for, again unlike the case with furniture, good silver fakers are very few, and they generally focus on potentially high-value pieces and opportunities for adding substantial value. Given the difficulties and costs of first securing proper genuine pieces for faking, then eliminating old marks, and finally making up an accurate and credible maker's-mark stamping punch, a silver faker needs a profit potential of at least 500 per cent to make silver faking worthwhile.

As I outlined in Chapter 3, except for Indian trade silver, the great majority of faked Canadian silver that I have so far seen or heard of has carried Quebec makers' marks – probably just because of value. Higher-value silver such as eighteenth-century church communion pieces, large plates, and domestic serving silver have so far been the fakers' favourites. Thus, any elaborate or expensive piece of silver, and particularly one with a well-known eighteenth- or early-nineteenth-century maker's punch-mark, deserves a thorough examination.

Iron

Fakes of antique iron, as discussed in Chapter 3, are now very widespread in the Canadian and American antiques market. The trouble with fake iron is that, properly made and corroded for an appearance of age, it is virtually identical to its antique counterparts and often difficult to identify as fake. Just for that reason, there is probably more fake ironwork now in the market than anyone realizes.

Fake blacksmith-made ironwork, from trivets to decorative hinges to fire tongs, is now being made in Southeast Asia as well as southern Europe. Most of this iron, because it is aimed at the huge North American market, duplicates or is very similar to North American antique pieces, which are often provided by importers and used as patterns.

Figs. 46, 46a: As perhaps the epitome of the faker's art, this silver plate combines a modern plate, an altered upgraded rim, and a fake maker's mark – all in the same piece. The supposed maker, Jean François Landron (1686–1759), was a New France-period Quebec silversmith, by whom about a dozen pieces are now known. The scalloped rim on the plate has been built up and reshaped, probably from an originally plain round rim. The curves and indentations of the rim, however, are inconsistent and not well finished.

The Landron ɪ*ꜰ over ʟ punch-mark (Fig. 46a) is distinct and crisp, hardly showing the wear and softening expected from two and a half centuries of polishing. The mark, though good, as with most fake marks from new punches, also differs in several details from Landron's original mark. The newly made punch was probably based on a drawing or photograph. The plate itself, though the rim is heavily altered, appears to be South American, originally unmarked, and twentieth century in date. *Private collection*

The prime points to look for with iron are modern details. Even the absence of these is no guarantee that a piece is early and genuine, however, but just that it may be a better-than-average fake. Look first at the metal. Blacksmith-made iron, from raw bars or scrap repeatedly heated and hammered, is typically irregular in shape and dimensions. To a calliper check, round sections are rarely absolutely round, nor are rectangular parts absolutely squared. Iron objects made from modern bar or strap metal, in spite of heating and hammering, are still likely to look like modern bar or strap. Few blacksmiths, producing fakes in quantity, are going to spend the time actually to change the shape of the metal, as opposed to simply forming it.

Another detail to check is the connections and joinings. Blacksmiths' welding is done by hammering together iron that is red- to white-hot from a forge. Blacksmith welds show hammer marks and often overlapping pieces of iron, but they are hammered smooth and do not require finish grinding. Modern electric or gas welding, while it is faster to accomplish, leaves excess metal and residue. In making fakes, that welding must be ground off flush, to try to hide the welds. Evidence of grinding marks, even under severe rusting, is also evidence of modern electric or oxygen-acetylene welding, and of modern fabrication.

Soldering of copper, brass, or tinned sheet iron should also be examined. Early soldering was done with hot soldering irons, used to melt lead to join the other metals. The resulting joints were often somewhat rough, and were then scraped, filed, or burnished smooth. Modern soldering is done with propane torches, which typically leave very smooth joints and little need for filing or polishing. Clearly, propane-torch soldering is evidence of modern manufacture – or at least modern repairs.

Early blacksmiths' rivets were also handmade, and show non-symmetrical and hot-hammered heading. Modern rivets usually have perfectly round and flat or semi-spherical heads.

Reproduction or fake cast iron (Fig. 36) is usually made from moulds, for which existing pieces are used as patterns. Cast iron is thus subject to the same loss of pattern detail and cooling shrinkage as anything else that is poured into a mould in a molten state, or as pottery, that requires firing and cooling. Modern cast iron also sometimes requires finish grinding of mould seams or casting overflows. With either blacksmith-made or cast iron, always look for signs of grinding, even under artificial rusting and corrosion.

Objects made of metals other than iron, including brass, are certainly less subject to outright fakery than silver, but inscriptions on such pieces still have to be watched. Many objects, such as brass compasses (Figs. 24, 24a) or swords (Fig. 22), would be difficult and uneconomic to fake completely as single items. There the much greater problem is the quantity of reproductions being produced, exactly as with the great quantities of blacksmith-made iron that are entering the antiques market.

Upgrading or add-on fakery of metals other than silver is usually limited to adding engraving on otherwise genuine pieces. Exactly as with makers' marks or inscriptions on silver, with inscriptions on other metals you must be able to answer the same questions: Is the inscription historically possible and accurate? Are engraved names or events accurate? Does a dated inscription correlate with the probable age of the piece on which it is engraved? Does the lettering or script style of the engraving also match the time period of the piece on which it is inscribed? Does the engraving or decoration appear to be contemporary with the object, done while the metal was smooth and clean, or was it done much later, after some object usage and possibly over corrosion or pitting? Anomalies anywhere are clues that the engraving may be suspicious.

Genuine name or presentation inscriptions, except on guns or swords, where they were common, were never typical on iron or steel. Silver was always preferred for presentations. Faked engraving is uncommon as well, compared to other forms of decoration, and on iron or steel most of the fakery also seems to be rather roughly done, either with an electric "vibro" tool or with a small hand-held jeweller's grinder. Much of this also misses on at least one of the elements of historical accuracy, lettering or script style, object versus engraving date, or engraving technique (Figs. 22–24).

Any object of decorated or engraved bone, tooth, tusk, or horn deserves automatic suspicion, for faking is rampant with everything from scrimshaw (described in Chapter 3) to powder horns. Because of very strict importation restrictions on whale products and elephant ivory, there is very little recent fakery *on the genuine organic material*, but a massive amount on look-alike plastics. Horn, however, is readily available, and thus we encounter many fake and recently carved powder horns. Any decoration or engraving should be subject to all of the questions that apply to silver and other metals.

Polymer and other plastic fakes, particularly decorative scrimshaw, pose a different problem. These are manufactured pieces, originally marketed as reproductions, though they get into the antiques market very quickly. They are not, however, reproductions of any known original pieces, but are invented designs carefully done in a nineteenth-century style.

The decorations of plastic fakes, however, typically have an unnatural sameness, with very even depth and width of incising and inscribing and very even colouring. Inscriptions, names, or dates are also subject to all the same errors of historical accuracy that often give away fake inscriptions on metals.

Two simple tests for polymer (or any) plastic fakes, or real bone or tusk, is a hot needle or fluorescence. A red-hot needle or pin tip, heated with just a match, will penetrate plastics or horn, but not bone or tooth. Likewise, under ultraviolet, or "black," light, real bone, tooth, or tusk will fluoresce or glow, while plastics do not. There are, however, also many known fakes, pieces recently done, on real organic materials, and judgements of fakery must be done stylistically.

Special attention should always be paid to pieces of silver or anything else engraved with inscriptions to famous or historically significant figures. Generally, inscriptions to or between people who are historical unknowns or very minor figures are genuine, because the engraved inscriptions add little if anything to the value of the pieces. This also applies to common family pieces, with inscriptions commemorating births, marriages, or whatever, as well as to trophies for accomplishments such as showing the best horse at a fair or winning a snowshoe race. These are typically genuine, for there is no economic reason for them not to be.

When we consider pieces with inscriptions to famous or well-known historical figures, however, we also encounter considerable past fakery. Whether on silver or swords (Fig. 22), firearms, brass (Fig. 24), or iron (Fig. 23), the inscriptions alone can create values well beyond those of the objects themselves. No doubt some such inscribed pieces may be quite genuine, for notable figures did of course receive inscribed gifts and formal presentations. Of all of those that emerge today, however, a large percentage have been faked at some time, sometimes even decades ago.

I could believe and accept an inscribed silver pitcher that read "To Samuel Shipbuilder on Completion of the Schooner *Helen A.*, 1845." It would be an interesting though not very significant piece of maritime history. Conversely, I would have great doubts about a pitcher inscribed "To Sir John A. MacDonald from President Abraham Lincoln, 1863." That, given events of the time and two factual mistakes in the inscription, would really be stretching credibility. The engraving would be fake.

Most gifts to notables from notables were also recorded in some way, whether with a certificate, in notes for a speech, in some letters, in meeting minutes or a resolution, as an entry in a diary, in a newspaper item, in a mention in a biography, or perhaps even by an original maker's or engraver's invoice. Thus, with any inscribed, and expensive, notable-to-notable presentation object, research into its background is essential. At least some documentation likely survives, somewhere. For a dealer or auction house, a well-researched and solid provenance for any antique also helps sell a piece and supports the price. To the buyer, the researched and solid provenance helps establish that the piece is genuine, and not faked.

Ceramics and Glass

As rock-hard materials formed by heat, pottery and glass are in a different category from wood, silver, brass, or other softer materials that are common candidates for upgrading or improvement fakery. Ceramics and glass are also quite fragile and subject to breakage, another risk for the would-be faker. Thus, opportunities for fakery that involve alteration of existing objects are limited pretty much to overpainting or overglazing, or attempting to remove museum or commercial reproduction markings.

Fakery or upgrading of otherwise genuine Canadian pottery and glass is quite uncommon. This is partly because of the difficulties of trying to alter and upgrade a hard, fragile material. In part, too, the values of most Canadian pottery and glass are not usually great enough to justify the effort.

Most of the fakery that has been tried on Canadian pottery – and none of it that I have seen is even remotely passable in a specialized collector market – has involved adding higher-valued decorations to otherwise plain pieces of salt-glazed stoneware. A crock or jug, maker-marked and with a cobalt-blue glazed decoration of a bird (Fig. 8), will be worth ten to twelve times the value of exactly the same salt-glazed piece unmarked and with no decoration. Fakers have occasionally made attempts to add blue decorations, usually with overglazing but sometimes even with paint, to otherwise genuine existing pieces, usually with ludicrous results (Fig. 8a).

The far greater problem with Canadian, and all, ceramics and glass is the appearance of reproductions or imported pieces described as Canadian in the antiques market. American and British reproduction glass, of virtually everything reproducible, has also flooded the Canadian market. European earthenware utility pottery, mostly nineteenth-century and perfectly genuine, has been imported in quantity and, posing as Canadian, now appears regularly in the Canadian antiques market.

In Canada, unlike the United States, very little antique glass or pottery has been reproduced – so far. Virtually all of those that have appeared have also been "museum" reproductions, which are typically well marked as what they are (Figs. 31, 37). English and European reproduction ceramics and glass, however, have been around for many decades (Appendix One), and most of them are unmarked.

We have to differentiate, with ceramics and glass, between hand-made pieces and moulded pieces. Handmade pieces are either free-blown, in the case of glass, or wheel-formed, in the case of ceramics.

Every handmade piece, both the original version and the reproduction, is somewhat different from every other, so there are no certain characteristics for measurements, colours, or decorations on which to base judgements. Comparison with known genuine pieces and wear, in the sense of scratching or chipping, can provide reasonable impressions and suppositions. Still, determining whether a piece of wheel-turned pottery or free-blown glass is genuine, fake, or reproduction can call for very subjective judgements. I have seen modern Mexican blown glass, aquamarine or pale-blue-green in colour, that I am sure could pass in some antiques markets as early-nineteenth-century New Jersey or New York glass, or Ontario Mallorytown glass. American blown glass has also been widely reproduced since the 1930s. Rather than "balance of probability" judgements, handmade ceramics and glass judgements very often cannot reliably get much beyond "balance of opinion."

Moulded ceramics or glass is blown, cast, or pressed using moulds or forms. The moulds are usually of iron for glass or of plaster of Paris or some other water-absorbent material for cast ceramics. Moulds impose standardizations of object sizes and decoration patterns, and moulded reproductions often change the materials or colours from the original versions (Fig. 37). Thus, moulded ceramics and glass have more definable characteristics to examine than do wheel-turned or free-blown pieces.

As outlined in Chapter 4, both glass and ceramics, like iron, are subject to slight shrinkage while cooling after moulding or kiln firing. Reproduction moulded glass can be made either from surviving original moulds or from new moulds made up using original glass objects as patterns. Reproduction glass cast from original moulds, of course, will be exactly the same, in size and patterns, as the originals. Unless it is known exactly what impurities were in the original glass, however, the colour even of "clear" glass will vary slightly between genuine pieces and reproductions, and is identifiable in side-by-side comparisons. Ring tones, because of differences in glass content, will vary as well. Many reproduction pieces have also been produced in colours that were never offered in original versions, making identification obvious (Fig. 37, bottom left).

New moulds, however carefully they are crafted and finished (an expensive proposition), are still never going to be precisely identical to the originals, nor is the reproduction glass that comes from them. To achieve absolute sameness, in dimensions, colours, and moulded patterns, between original antique glass and reproductions from new moulds would be virtually impossible.

The Royal Ontario Museum reproduction "Rayed Heart" goblets (Fig. 37) required a new mould. The resulting goblet differs in dimensions, as well as in glass content, from the original. The content difference in turn affects colour match and ring tone. There are also many small anomalies in the moulded pattern itself. Thus, side-by-side comparison, or often even comparison with published photographs, will usually show up the inevitable subtle differences between genuine and reproduction moulded or "pressed" glass.

Original plaster moulds for antique cast or pressed ceramics were fragile, and few still survive. Consequently, reproductions require new moulds. The moulds, of plaster or other absorbent material, are usually formed directly, by pressing the mould material around an existing and genuine piece and then removing it in sections. This will create a mould of exactly the same size as the original pattern piece. The reproduction that is cast from that mould and then fired, however, will always be slightly smaller than the original piece because of cooling shrinkage.

Decorative patterns in ceramics, as with anything else where moulds are copied from original pieces as patterns, always lose detail. Thus, patterns in reproduction moulded pottery are typically less distinct than the originals. Modern clays, of precisely known components and firing temperatures, are far more consistent in content than natural clays that were dug, cleaned of dirt and stones, and fired by temperature guess in the nineteenth century. Modern slips and glazes, used in reproductions, are also of quite different content from the natural metallic-oxide colourings of nineteenth-century glazes. The toxic lead-oxide glazes used on nineteenth-century pottery have also been banned in North America for nearly a century.

Beyond simple add-on decorations (Fig. 8a), any potter trying to create truly passable fakes would have to go back to nineteenth-century methods and materials, using natural clay, lead glazes, and a wood-fuelled kiln. Few would-be pottery fakers would go to that much trouble. Therefore, most fake Canadian pottery turns out to have started life as reproductions, or as antique imports from Europe. Though clay body and glaze colouring may be consistent, older pottery reproductions may also show wear and use, or even old chips, the result of sometimes deliberate antiquing.

Most of the intentional and deliberate fakery found in Canadian antiques focuses on furniture, particularly pine furniture, and to a lesser extent on silver, particularly church and domestic table silver. Both are quite common. Nothing, however, is immune from faking or fakery.

In spite of the constant production of new fakes and upgrading fakery, reproductions still remain the greater and most rapidly growing problem. Although fakes and fakery may be produced by the dozens or hundreds, every object still involves individual skill and effort. Reproductions, however, are turned out by the thousands, usually in small factories rather than craft shops. Some, such as Indian trade silver, scrimshaw, pressed glass, or blacksmith-made iron, are made specifically for the collector market and are commonly distributed through antiques dealers and shows.

Other reproductions, including everything from furniture to pewter and from stoneware pottery to Tiffany-style leaded-glass lampshades, are intended for the more general decor-oriented market. Promotion and distribution is generally done through magazine advertising and catalogues. There have actually been articles in home-decorating magazines on people who custom-built reproduction seventeenth- or eighteenth-century houses and then furnished them entirely with reproductions of seventeenth- or eighteenth-century furniture, paintings and prints, pottery, glass, fireplace ironwork, or whatever. With the present range of reproductions available, it would not be difficult to create a quite realistic historical and antique image and decor without any true antiques at all.

After one or two changes of hands, however, some of these reproductions invariably begin to appear in Definition-3 antique shows or
in dealers' shops. Once a reproduction, perhaps twenty years or half a
century down the line, gains the status of "antique," like my mother's
sideboard, that status can continue forever until – or unless – a piece
is re-identified. Reproductions are even now being advertised as "future
antiques" or "future heirlooms" rather than FutureFakes, and lectures
are offered on the investment potential of both "future antiques" and
manufactured "collectibles." The lectures, of course, are often spon-
sored by manufacturers or distributors with a strong sales motivation.

Future antiquarians may actually be facing three separate levels of
"antiques." We will have, first, the existing Definition-1 or "pure age"
antique, the true-blue genuine article, made during the pre-industrial
craft period. Next we will have the first wave or age of reproductions,
reasonably exact copies, often at least partially made by craft-period
methods, of roughly the 1880s through the 1920s. Finally, then, we will
have the present and third level, widely advertised "future heirlooms,"
produced since 1945 and largely since 1960.

With the third level has also come a strong craft revival, which has
created a huge cottage industry in both the United States and Canada.
Hundreds or perhaps thousands of individual cabinetmakers, potters,
glass blowers and moulders, blacksmiths, silver and pewter makers,
weavers, and other craftspeople are now busily producing and marketing reproductions. Even a cursory glance through a magazine such
as *Early American Life* will outline the size, scale, and infinite variety
of the reproduction industry.

The problem for antiquarians fifty years or a century hence will
arise from the fact that in many cases the contemporary craftspeople
are every bit as skilled and proficient, or more, than their seventeenth-
through nineteenth-century predecessors, and they certainly are far
better equipped. Anyone who thinks that age-old craft technology or
extreme skill, backed by modern equipment, has vanished after a
century and a half of industrialization is dead wrong. Not all reproductions show mass-market or low-cost adaptations. Some are
superlative.

For the antiquarian, specialist collector, or antiques dealer, the potential impact of the better reproductions and the "future heirlooms" is mind-boggling. No one could begin to list or catalogue, even now, everything that is being or has been reproduced, for the sands shift too quickly.

There are virtually always small visual differences and clues that separate fakes and reproductions from original and genuine antiques. Whether the construction of furniture, the styles and markings of silver and metals, or the clays, glazes, and decorations of pottery, every reproduction, in little details, can be separated from older and original pieces.

No one can presume to know everything. Most dedicated collectors and many dealers, however, are at least somewhat specialized in their preferences and subjects. As in any other field, from computers to surgery to engine repairs, increasing complexity makes specialization essential, in order to gain the experience and depth of knowledge necessary to navigate the fake- and reproduction-filled antiques market.

Observation, knowledge, and experience are, of course, requisite to survival. In the future, however, there will likely be ever fewer generalists. Someone expert in antique furniture, including fakes and reproductions, will be unlikely to have also the same expertise with silver, or iron, or with ceramics and glass. Few do even now. On balance, it is probably better for a collector or dealer today to gain a deep knowledge of a specialized subject than, at best, a superficial knowledge of the whole antiques spectrum.

The whole broad field of antiques collecting is not only a jungle, but a jungle with a constantly expanding and constantly shifting landscape. It is also a field so infinite and so diverse that it defies any precise definition, and in the end comes down to ultimate individuality. Though the objects, the antiques, are the commodity and the motivation, collecting and the antiques market is really about people. The expert, the knowledgeable, the ignorant, and the foolish, as well as the honest, the shady, and the crooked, combined with the careful, the profligate, and the truly obsessed, are people all in the same game, all at the same time. I could not think of any other field with such a mix of competing and inter-reacting personalities, preferences, goals, or even personal insanities, than collecting and the antiques market. That is the core, perhaps, of what makes antiques collecting all so much fun.

U.S. Consular Notice of 1909

The production of antique fakes in Britain and Europe, aimed at the North American market, was not nearly as extensive before the First World War as it became in the 1920s and 1930s and the post-Second World War period. Still, even as of 1909, fakery was rampant, enough so as to justify the following cautions from the American Consul in Edinburgh, Scotland. Because so many of these fakes also made their way to Canada, I've included this report as a present-day caution. Everything mentioned in this report is still out there – somewhere. The warning was published in the *United States Daily Consular Trade Reports, 1909,* and is quoted verbatim below:

The United States is reputed by the well-informed to harbor more "artistic atrocities" that were purchased as genuine than any other country in the world, and we may see even a greater flux of pseudo works of art in American stores unless these frauds are detected by government experts or rejected by public taste. The purpose of this article is to state facts, not opinions, and it is not addressed to the experienced collector. A real service, however, may possibly be conferred by warning the inexperienced – those who perhaps go abroad for the first time and find the curiosity shops places of interest, and many of whom doubtless can little afford to be so heavily penalized for their credulity by antique dealers.

Just now miniatures and decorated snuff and matchboxes are being most extensively collected by Americans. These and other such small "articles of vertu" are manufactured by dexterous copyists and are readily procurable by the gross. No one not possessing knowledge of the subject, great experience, and discrimination should ever allow himself to be tempted to purchase miniatures unless he is content to possess a cabinet of forgeries. The vast quantities of bijouterie, Dresden and Battersea enamel ware that is just now flooding the market is made on the Continent, principally for the American trade. Apart from the painting on these, which is poor in quality and generally a crude copy of some original example, if one will observe closely it will be revealed that the rim to which the top is hinged is artificially colored and that the evidence of fresh glue extending from underneath is a further betrayal of its modern and hazy origin.

The collection of china, likewise, must inevitably lead the novice to an even more hopeless plight. Genuine examples of Dresden, Chelsea, Worcester or Bow are worth more than their weight in gold; yet what one may fondly imagine to be a convincing piece, with its refined decoration and simple gilding, bearing the golden anchor, is not a bit of old Chelsea, but a "fake" made by well-known firms on the Continent. Only the uninitiated now put any reliance in "old marks." They are meaningless, and are freely applied to modern copies with open and notorious forgery. There are occasionally some rare pieces of china and pottery yet to be procured, as well as genuine examples of the more recent periods of some of the notable factories (usually early nineteenth century), such as Derby, Worcester, Spode, Coalport, and Rockingham China and Wedgwood, Mason and other Staffordshire potteries. These may possess some slight sentimental and antique value, and are well worth buying for practical use, but in themselves they cannot be called fine and are otherwise unworthy of collection. But even then such pieces should be purchased only under expert advice and with a written guaranty of genuineness.

With reference to the effectiveness of the written guaranty the English courts have recently sustained the contention that if a false description of an antique is given in the invoice, the purchaser is entitled to full recovery. The written guaranty is therefore far from being valueless and should always be insisted on as a protection. Furthermore, any evasion or hesitation on the part of the dealer to give one should be accepted as a token of his dishonesty.

Before leaving the subject of china it might be stated that Cromwellian coins [1650s] of small denomination, wholly worthless [as of 1909] to the numismatic collector, bring from ten to fifteen times their face value among purveyors of "fake" antiques, since they can be imbedded in a tray or the bottom of a punch or toddy ladle to convince the gullible of the genuineness of his purchase.

The forger of old English silver has been somewhat restrained by fear of the law, which makes the sophistication of hallmarks in Great Britain a very hazardous occupation. Likewise, the almost prohibitive prices for which early English silver is offered confine its collection, generally speaking, to connoisseurs. The ingenuity of the faker, however, is none the less occasionally exercised to insert into some late piece of modern copy old marks taken from an article of little value. Beyond the actual intrinsic value of the metal, specimens of the late Georgian period are worthless [as of 1909], yet they are now being extensively collected by many dealers throughout Great Britain for sale to American customers, who willingly pay from ten to twenty times their trade value.

It is a difficult undertaking to dispel the threefold illusion that old Sheffield plate is to be found almost anywhere in the United Kingdom; that it is as valuable as silver of the same period; and the genuine can easily be detected from the spurious by the fact that it has a discernible sub-surface of copper. Now the truth of the latter is that much modern electroplate is done on a copper body, as was the case with the old. The precise difference, however, between the old and the new is that, with respect to the former, the silver was first fused and beaten on to a copper block, the whole slug afterwards being worked into shape by hand; whereas, after the discovery of electroplating in 1840 or thereabouts, the article to be silvered was mechanically evolved and the silver instantaneously applied by the electro process. The results of these two methods are vastly dissimilar, for instead of the play and incidence of light on the beaten and uneven surface, which imparts one of the chief charms to the handwrought process, there is, when the silver has been mechanically applied, only an assertiveness and garish regularity of surface. Genuine Old Sheffield plate in its original and unrenovated condition is worth about 80 per cent as much as modern silver and about 25 per cent of silver of a contemporary period. It is, however, worth five or six times the commercial value of "faked" Sheffield plate, with which in no other way can a comparison be made. Literally tons of faked Sheffield plate are now being manufactured, most of which, sooner or later, finds its way to America and the colonies [such as Canada].

With respect to pewter, the love for which did not assert itself until long after most of it had disappeared in the melting pot, it might safely be said that 95 per cent of all one could find through England and Scotland has been made within the last ten years. Likewise, practically all of the "Old Dutch" brass articles, such as alms dishes, plaques, candlesticks, and jardinieres are of modern make, although they may reach the dealer via Holland. The production of "old masters" and ancestors continues a lucrative industry in Great Britain, it being a matter for serious regret that the talent, and sometimes even genius, suggested by these fraudulent works of art should be abased to such mean ends.

Difficulties thicken as the subject of old English furniture is approached. Large stakes are here frequently played for and the cunning of the dealer amounts to sheer genius. Illustrative of this, an instance of recent occurrence may be cited. What purported to be some exceptionally rare Chippendale chairs were sold by a well-known dealer to a certain nobleman, Lord X, who unhesitatingly accepted the dealer's word that they were genuine. Some time after this, however, the services of an expert were employed to further examine them, when it was revealed that a swindle had been perpetrated, the chairs being nothing more than fine copies. The customer informed the dealer of this discovery, demanding, on penalty of exposure, that the full purchase price be immediately refunded. Much to the purchaser's surprise, the dealer refused to make restitution under circumstances which he alleged involved both his reputation and his honor. But to put it differently, if the customer would simply state his dissatisfaction with his purchase, then he (the dealer), knowing the chairs to be genuine, would thank him for the privilege of being allowed to recover them, but it must be distinctly understood, only upon the terms and conditions of an ordinary sale. The dealer thereupon offered about $1,000 over and above the sum for which the chairs had previously been purchased. To this, of course, the nobleman demurred, protesting that he desired no profit from an unfortunate venture, but in the end, in order to secure the recovery of his money, he was prevailed upon to acquiesce in this extraordinary proposal.

The chairs having been duly returned, no great time elapsed before another customer took their purchase under consideration. The sale had now, however, become much simplified, for not only could the source of purchase be pointed to with pride, but actually the check was exhibited, showing beyond all doubt that the chairs had been purchased from Lord X, the well-known collector, at a price indicative of their apparent worth. Thus the dealer, shadowing his own dishonesty by this clever ruse, contrived to snatch even a further profit out of this second and more unscrupulous transaction.

It is no exaggeration to say that such episodes are a daily occurrence in the antique trade, except that, generally speaking, the ignorant seldom gets in exchange for his investment even so much as a good modern copy. Many so-called antique shops actually carry on business without having one genuine piece of antique furniture in their establishment.

In Holland old chests, cabinets, desks and chairs of little value are collected and, after being veneered with cheaply made marquetry, are sent to Great Britain. Old oak beams from demolished churches or granaries are likewise in constant demand for conversion into Jacobean refectory tables and Queen Anne furniture. Mid-Victorian pedestal sideboards are amputated to speci-mens of Robert Adam, and conventional inlay suitable for Sheraton furniture is cut out by machinery and supplied in any quantity to those who have skill and inclination to fabricate antiques. Grandfather clocks are frequently made up of such incongruities as a modern dial with a forged maker's name and date, an old case patched up and set off by modern inlay, and perhaps works of about fifty years ago. Grandfather chairs are also, almost without excep-tion, modern or old frames debauched by new cabriole or claw-and-legs. Violins signed Stradivarius or Jacobus Stainer, surreptitiously hidden in rubbish heaps, are replaced by others as soon as sold. "Old" armours, medals and medallions, all of modern origin, abound in rich profusion. "Antique" Spanish, Portuguese and English paste jewelry everywhere intrudes itself. A flood of cheap and inartistic Japanese ware is also pouring out over the country; prints, gold lacquer, cloisonné enamel, ivory, and bronze contribut-ing a full share in the swelling volume of alloys and commercial antiques.

To successfully collect nowadays requires expert knowledge and technical training. Therefore, those who wish to secure genuine antiques would be better to make up their minds that it will be more satisfactory, and cheaper in the end, to purchase only on expert advice or of dealers willing to give a written stipulation that all articles sold are guaranteed to be approximately of the period represented; and with respect to English furniture, that no carving, inlay or repairs not frankly admitted have been added; purchase money to be refunded should any of these statements prove on examination to be untrue. Furthermore, the services of this office [American Consulate, Edinburgh] are at the disposal of any person wishing more specific and detailed advice.

Glossary of Antiques Market Terms

Every profession or business develops its own language and jargon, and the antiques world is no different. The language is also changeable. "Collectible," for example, is a fairly recent term. Terms also differ somewhat between countries, or regionally, so that common descriptive words in one area of North America may be uncommon or unknown in another region. "Tarting up," meaning cleaning and superficial restoration, is a more common American than Canadian term; we tend to say "cleaning up." Something like "catywhompus," a Maine and northern New England term for something bent, twisted, crushed, or broken, is a regional term unknown in Canada.

The entire English language, spoken and written worldwide, has many dialects and is in constant flux. Thus, the following glossary is of antiques-market terms current as of this writing. I have not included "catywhompus," and there are likely other regional terms, used only within their own areas, which are also not included.

absentee bid (or **left bid** or **order bid**): An advance bid left with an auction house by a bidder who does not plan to attend the auction. Higher absentee bids will be used by the auctioneer against floor bids. An absentee bid will be successful, sometimes below its limit, if it tops the highest floor bid.

advance: Auctioneers, from their **openers,** call bids to auction audiences, with bidders responding with silent signals or by holding up a numbered card. Following each bidder response, the auctioneer then advances the bid to a higher figure. The amounts of bid advances are entirely at the auctioneer's discretion. A piece is then sold to the highest bidder when no higher bid advance can gain a buyer response.

antique (verb): Artificially aging a fake or reproduction by creating an appearance of wear and use. Antiquing, or distressing, can call for many techniques, from rubbing wear spots on painted pine reproduction furniture to tea-staining paper to simulate age-fading.

Attribute; attribution: An expert opinion on the probable maker or place of origin of an antique. An attribution, to be credible, should be by a recognized authority on the type of object being attributed and should always be in writing.

authenticate: A term often used by individuals who own objects and are seeking an opinion that their piece is genuine and good. Authenticate is not a term typically used by collectors, dealers, or auction houses, but more commonly by owners or would-be buyers. People asking an expert to authenticate an object are often seeking confirmation of what they already believe.

breaker: A piece of furniture either in such poor condition or missing so many parts that, financially and in time or effort, it is not worth the cost or work of restoring. Breakers, or junkers, are usually kept to provide parts or old wood for other restorations or for **made-up** fakes.

brush out: To acquire a piece that has never before been in the antiques market or been owned by a collector or dealer. Objects are typically brushed out from original locations or long-term owners, usually by **pickers**.

buy in: An auction-house term for unsold. An object at auction that fails to attract bids of at least the reserve price set by the seller is bought in and removed from sale by the auctioneer, for return to the consignor. Though the piece is not sold, the consignor is still charged the seller's commission based on the reserve price.

cherry-pick: In the sale of an entire collection, to choose, or cherry-pick, selectively and buy – or try to buy – only the best or most desirable pieces. The seller of a collection who allows buyers to cherry-pick will usually sell the best, but wind up with no one taking the least desirable pieces.

clean up: See **tart up**.

collectible: A recent term for manufactured objects that are usually modern or newly made, not antique, but that are widely collected. The term can also include many Definition-3 semi-antique **smalls**, or small objects. Newly manufactured collectibles are heavily advertised by their marketers and promoters, and include everything from "limited-edition" decaled "collector" plates to private mint productions and from dolls to "proof" coin sets. These collectibles are a producer-promoter commodity, but there is as yet little secondary (auction-antiques dealer) market for them. Older collectibles can be any obsolete but not quite antique objects (defined by age), from matchbooks to commemorative china – virtually anything that anyone may choose to collect.

commission, buyer's: A surcharge commission, typically 10 per cent or sometimes 15 per cent, which art and antiques auction houses charge to buyers, adding the buyers' commission to final sale prices. With buyers' commissions plus sales taxes added, final auction costs to buyers in Canada are roughly a quarter more than final bid, or **hammer**, prices. Rural auctioneers typically charge high **sellers'** commissions, but do not try to levy buyers' commissions as well.

commission, seller's: The commission an auction house charges and withholds for selling a piece at auction. Sellers' commissions are typically a $75 or $100 minimum, up to 10 per cent to 20 per cent (or even 25 per cent without a **buyer's commission**) of the sale price. The commission is deducted from what is finally paid to the seller.

distress (verb): See **antique**.

divorced: One or both sections of an original two-section piece that have had new bases or tops applied, transforming them into individual free-standing pieces. Divorced pieces with new tops or bases are fakes. Divorced is the opposite of **married**.

dog: An object that is in either extremely poor condition or has been so upgraded, faked, or over-restored, or is so common in the antiques market that it is effectively unsaleable.

estate sale; estate auction: A term for an auction supposedly selling the object contents of an estate of a named person, and often used to establish **provenance**. Additional auctioneer-owned pieces (see **salting**) are commonly added to estate sales, but are only rarely indicated or announced as such. Estate sales can be wholly invented, composed of objects actually owned by the auctioneer or unknown consignors, but be advertised as being the estate contents even of someone who never actually existed. "Estate" used just as an adjective, as in "estate jewellery" or "estate furniture," has no more meaning than other adjectives such as "important" or "rare."

estimate: Auction-house term for the high and low spreads of prices an auction house thinks pieces will bring at auction. High and low estimates are published in auction catalogues, and though actual bidding may fall low or high of estimates, they guide the bidding, which often ends within the estimated range. Auctions held without catalogues do not offer estimates.

hammer price; knock-down price: An auctioneer, on accepting the last bid and closing bidding, raps the podium with a gavel or wooden block, or says, "Sold," indicating the lot is sold at that price. If the lot has not met its **reserve price** and is unsold, the auctioneer may still rap as if it was, but not actually announce, "Sold."

improve; improvements; upgrade; upgrading: To substantially alter an object with decorations or additions that were not part of the original object. Improvement, or upgrading, is a form of fakery. With furniture, improvement can be simply the replacement of original wooden knobs with reproduction brasses, adding carving (Figs. 10, 16, 17), or even changing of case shapes (Figs. 6, 7, 11).

in the rough: Any antique in well-used, battered, or unrestored condition, as-found but unsaleable as it is. A piece found in the rough will be restored, be **tarted up**, or be kept and stored as a **breaker** or **junker**.

junker: See **breaker**.

made-up: An object, usually but not always furniture, fabricated from parts of one or more other objects (see **breaker; junker**), typically mixed with other new work of old wood or material (Fig. 15). Made-up pieces are fakes.

married: A two-sectioned object fabricated from separate upper and lower sections, taken from previously different pieces and fitted and blended to match, such as the secretary-desk in Figure 14 or the two-tiered buffet in Figure 15. Married pieces are fakes. Married is the opposite of **divorced**.

museum reproduction: A reproduction produced or authorized by a museum. Museum reproductions are usually carefully checked by curators and/or expert committees and are the most nearly identical to original objects. These reproductions nearly always carry a museum name or logo (Figs. 31, 34–37), but those markings are not always impervious to tampering.

off-the-wall bid; phantom bid: A non-existent bid in an auction. An auctioneer with only one actual bidder, in attempting to bid up the price of an object, may announce a fictional phantom bid or accept a bid off the wall. A variation is having a **shill** in the audience actually making bids. A good auctioneer can usually conceal and get away with this, but runs the risk of the real bidder dropping out, leaving the object unsold.

opener; opening bid: The amount at which an auctioneer opens the call for bids, usually below or at a seller's **reserve price**. The auctioneer has discretion over openers as well as bid **advances**.

picker; to pick: A first-discovery-level dealer who picks, buying directly from original households or long-term owners (see **brush out**). Pickers typically sell pieces they have picked, or brushed out, to retail dealers or through rural auctions.

plant; to plant: An agent, often a third party, used for the initial sale of fakes or faked pieces into the antiques market through pickers, dealers, or auctions. A plant is neither a faker nor a buyer, but serves as a buffer to prevent planted fakes being traced back to their creators.

preview: An advance public showing or display of objects to be included in an auction sale. The preview may be on the same day as the sale, and just prior to it, or it may be one or two days in advance. At upper-level auction houses, the preview may be combined with an invitational reception for prospective bidders.

provenance: The known past history of an antique. Though provenance can go back to the origins of a piece, that is now rare. Provenance is most usually limited to more recent recorded ownership, collections, exhibitions, or prior sales. Verbal provenances are often embellished or pure fiction, and for credibility must suggest a history that matches the period of the object itself, and be reasonably checkable.

reserve: An auction term for the price the seller has indicated is the least he/she will accept – usually 20 to 40 per cent below the low estimate published in the catalogue. Where bidding for a piece does not meet the reserve price, the auctioneer **buys in** the object for return to the consignor. An auction, or specific pieces, offered without sellers' reserve prices, is called unreserved. Unreserved auctions, however, may be manipulated, with the auctioneer getting his price by using **off-the-wall** bids or a **shill**.

salt; salting: A term with two uses. Dealers with a large quantity of objects of very low value may offer multiple-item deals, salting the multiple items with a few slightly more valuable items. A coin dealer, for example, might put out a box of basically worthless coins, offered at ten coins for $8, and salt the box with a few coins worth $1 or $2 each as bait for buyers. Auctioneers, as well, will often salt an advertised **estate** sale with their own added pieces, or with consignments from **pickers** or from fakers' **plants**. The **estate-sale** cover provides past-ownership **provenance** and a suggestion of originality, with bidders not aware that **wrong**, or faked, pieces, though not part of the estate property, may have been salted into the sale.

shill: A person planted in an auction audience to make false bids in an attempt to boost prices. The shill might be a relative or employee of the auctioneer, but the person and any relationship must be unknown to the auction audience. Use of a shill is a substitute for an auctioneer taking **phantom** bids **off the wall**.

sleeper: A severely underpriced object, otherwise a genuine bargain. A sleeper can emerge either because a **picker** or dealer has acquired it for far less than market value, and/or the real value of the object has gone unrecognized. The Nisbet table in Figure 5, if it was found for $100 in an old barn, would be a real sleeper.

smalls: A dealer term for small items such as pottery and chinaware, glass, figurines, or other small objects. A dealer, in a shop or packing for an antiques show, can offer or take far more smalls than furniture.

tart up; clean up: Cosmetic preparation for sale. Tarting up an object does not involve either extensive restoration or improvement, but usually just a superficial tightening or glueing of loose parts or joints, and cleaning, polishing, or waxing. Tarting up can also include simple **improvement**, such as replacing hardware.

theme sale: An auction term for a sale of large concentrations or collections of a very few types of objects. An antique-silver theme sale, for example, will attract numerous bidder-buyers primarily interested in silver, which will (it is hoped) increase bidding competition and raise prices. Theme sales tend to be more dealer-dominated than general sales.

upgrade: See **improve**.

vet; vetted: A term applied to better antique shows, with a knowledgeable committee which checks, or vets, each dealer's offerings before the show opening. Vetting teams have discretion to weed out and order removal of questionable or faked pieces, or pieces that are of too recent a date for the show's guidelines. Larger and charitable antiques shows are usually vetted, while promoters' shows usually are not.

wrong; funny: A judgement of intuition and experience, though perhaps based on uncertain hard evidence. An object that rings cautionary bells and just doesn't appear as it should, but that does not necessarily have anything definite that one can immediately point to, is a piece that seems wrong. The sense that something is wrong or funny is a hunch or feeling, though not necessarily a provable fact.

yawner: An evening auction, with too many small lots and a slow-moving auctioneer, that goes on into the wee hours of the morning. A Webster's Law of yawners is that pieces you came to bid on come up for sale only toward the end of the auction.

Fakes & Fakery

Arnau, Frank [pseud.]. *The Art of the Faker.* Boston: Little Brown, 1961.

Bly, John, ed. *Is it Genuine? How to Collect Antiques with Confidence.* Toronto: Stoddart, 1986.

Broad, W. & Wade, N. *Betrayers of the Truth.* Oxford Univ. Press, 1985.

Cescinsky, Herbert. *The Gentle Art of Faking Furniture.* London: Chapman & Hall, 1931. Reprint. New York: Dover, 1967.

Cole, Sonya. *Counterfeit.* London, 1955.

Constable, W. G. *Forgers and Forgeries.* New York: Harry N. Abrams, 1954.

Corning Museum of Glass. *True or False?* Exhibition Catalogue, Corning, N.Y., 1953.

Dutton, Denis. *The Forger's Art.* Berkeley: Univ. of Calif., 1983.

Frank, Stuart M. *Fakeshaw: A Checklist of Plastic "Scrimshaw."* Sharon, Mass.: Kendall Whaling Museum, 1993.

Goodbar, Richard L. *Fakes and Forgeries, Marriages and Deceptions.* Hunt Valley Antiques Show Catalogue, 1984.

Hamilton, Charles. *Great Forgers and Famous Fakes.* New York, 1980.

Hammond, Dorothy. *Confusing Collectibles: A Guide to the Identification of Reproductions.* Leon, Iowa: Mid-America, 1969.

——. *Confusing Collectibles: A Guide to the Identification of Contemporary Objects.* Des Moines, Iowa: Wallace-Homestead, 1979.

Hayward, Charles H. *Antique or Fake? How to Recognize Real Antiques.* London: Evans. Reprint. Toronto: Coles, 1977.

Hoving, Thomas. *False Impressions: The Hunt for Big-Time Art Fakes.* New York: Simon & Schuster, 1996.

Jenks, Bill; Luna, Jerry; & Reilly, Darryl. *Identifying Pattern Glass Reproductions.* Radnor, Pa.: Wallace-Homestead, 1993.

Jeppson, Lawrence. *Fabulous Frauds.* London, 1971.

Jones, Mark, ed. *Fake? The Art of Deception.* Exhibition Catalogue, London: British Museum, 1990.

Kaye, Myrna. *Fake, Fraud, or Genuine? Identifying Authentic American Antique Furniture.* Boston: Little Brown, 1987.

Kurz, Otto. *Fakes.* London: Faber & Faber, 1948. Reprint. New York: Dover, 1967.

Lee, Ruth Webb. *Antique Fakes and Reproductions.* Wellesley Hills, Mass.: Lee Pubs., 1950.

Minneapolis Institute of Arts. *Fakes and Forgeries.* Exhibition Catalogue, Minneapolis, 1973.

Nobili, R. *The Gentle Art of Faking.* London, 1922.

Orvell, Miles. *The Real Thing: Imitation and Authenticity in American Culture, 1880–1940.* Chapel Hill, N.C.: Univ. of North Carolina, 1989.

Peterson, Harold L. *How to Tell If It's a Fake.* New York: Scribner's, 1975.

Phillips, David. *Don't Trust the Label.* London Arts Council, Exhibition Catalogue, 1986.

Sachs, Samuel II. *Fakes and Forgeries.* Exhibition Catalogue, Minneapolis Institute of Art, 1973.

Savage, George. *Forgeries, Fakes, and Reproductions.* London, 1976.

Schuller, Sepp. *Forgers, Dealers, Experts.* London, 1960.

Theus, Will H. *How to Detect and Collect Antique Furniture.* New York: Knopf, 1978.

Yale University. *The Eye of the Beholder: Fakes, Replicas and Alteration in American Art.* Exhibition Catalogue, Yale University Art Gallery, 1977.

Yates, Raymond F. *Antique Fakes and Their Detection.* New York: Harper & Row, 1950.

Young, Norman. *Fabulous but Fake.* Albany, N.Y.: Fake Publications, 1993.

Canadian Antiques

The following includes only selected general and broad-spectrum Canadian antiques books, but not localized, individual maker or factory, or archaeological titles.

Furniture:

Bird, Michael. *Canadian Country Furniture, 1675-1950.* Toronto: Stoddart-Boston Mills, 1994.

Dobson, Henry and Barbara. *The Early Furniture of Ontario and the Atlantic Provinces.* Toronto: M. F. Feheley, 1974.

Foss, Charles. *Cabinetmakers of the Eastern Seaboard.* Toronto: M. F. Feheley, 1977.

MacLaren, George. *Antique Furniture by Nova Scotian Craftsmen.* Toronto: McGraw Hill-Ryerson, 1961.

——. *Nova Scotia Furniture.* Halifax: Petheric Press, 1969.

Pain, Howard. *The Heritage of Upper Canadian Furniture.* Toronto: Van Nostrand-Reinhold, 1978.

Palardy, Jean. *The Early Furniture of French Canada.* Toronto: Macmillan, 1963.

Ryder, Huia. *Antique Furniture by New Brunswick Craftsmen.* Toronto: Ryerson Press, 1965.

Shackleton, Philip. *The Furniture of Old Ontario.* Toronto: Macmillan, 1978.

Webster, Donald. *English-Canadian Furniture of the Georgian Period.* Toronto: McGraw Hill-Ryerson, 1979.

Ceramics; Pottery:

Collard, Elizabeth. *Nineteenth-Century Pottery and Porcelain in Canada.* Montreal: McGill Univ. Press, 1967.

——. *The Potters' View of Canada.* Kingston: McGill-Queens Univ. Press, 1983.

Newlands, David. *Early Ontario Potters; Their Craft and Trade.* Toronto: McGraw Hill-Ryerson, 1979.

Webster, Donald. *Early Canadian Pottery.* Toronto: McClelland & Stewart, 1971.

——. *Decorated Stoneware Pottery of North America.* Tokyo: Charles E. Tuttle, 1971.

Glass:

Bird, Douglas and Marion; Corke, Charles. *A Century of Canadian Glass Fruit Jars.* London, Ont.: privately published, 1971.

King, Thomas. *Glass in Canada.* Erin, Ont.: Boston Mills Press, 1987.

MacLaren, George. *Nova Scotia Glass.* Halifax: Nova Scotia Museum, 1968.

Stevens, Gerald. *Early Canadian Glass.* Toronto: Ryerson Press, 1960.

Spence, Hilda and Kevin. *A Guide to Early Canadian Glass.* Toronto: Longmans, 1966.

——. *Glass in Canada: The First One Hundred Years.* Toronto: Methuen, 1982.

Unitt, Doris and Peter. *Treasury of Canadian Glass.* Peterborough, Ont.: Clock House, 1969.

———. *American and Canadian Goblets.* 2 vols., Peterborough: Clock House, 1974.

———. *Bottles in Canada.* Peterborough: Clock House, 1972.

Silver:

Derome, Robert. *Les Orfevres de Nouvelle-France.* Ottawa: National Gallery of Canada, 1974.

Langdon, John. *Canadian Silversmiths, 1700-1900.* Lunenburg, Vermont: privately published, 1960.

———. *Canadian Silversmiths and their Marks, 1667-1867.* Lunenburg, Vermont: privately published, 1966.

MacKay, Donald. *Silversmiths and Related Craftsmen of the Atlantic Provinces.* Halifax: Petheric Press, 1973.

Traquair, Ramsay. *The Old Silver of Quebec.* Toronto: Macmillan, 1940.

Trudel, Jean. *L'Orfeverie en Nouvelle-France.* Ottawa: National Gallery of Canada, 1974.

Trees and Woods:

Fowells, H. A. *Silvics of Forest Trees of the United States.* Washington: U. S. Forest Service, 1965.

Hosie, R. C. *Native Trees of Canada.* Ottawa: Canadian Forestry Service, 1969.

Lauriault, Jean. *Identification Guide to the Trees of Canada.* Markham, Ont.: Fitzhenry & Whiteside, 1989.

Miscellany:

Abrahamson, Una. *God Bless Our Home: Domestic Life in Nineteenth-Century Canada.* Toronto: Burns & MacEachern, 1966.

Burrows, G. Edmund. *Canadian Clocks and Clockmakers.* Oshawa, Ont.: privately published, 1973.

Hume, Ivor Noel. *All the Best Rubbish.* New York: Harper & Row, 1974.

Lessard, Michel, and Marquis, Hugette. *Complete Guide to French-Canadian Antiques.* New York: Hart, 1974.

Miller, Steve. *The Art of the Weathervane.* Exton, Pa.: Shiffer, 1984.

Minhinnick, Jean. *At Home in Upper Canada.* Toronto: Clarke Irwin, 1970.

Smith, Charles W. *Auctions. The Social Construction of Value.* New York: Free Press-Macmillan, 1989.

Smith, Jean and Elizabeth. *Collecting Canada's Past.* Scarborough, Ont.: Prentice Hall, 1974.

Webster, Donald. *The Book of Canadian Antiques.* Toronto: McGraw Hill-Ryerson, 1974.

INDEX

Figures and their captions are indicated in **bold**.